GREENHOUSE GARDENING IN COLOUR

WHSMITH

Greenhouse Gardening in Colour

William Davidson

this edition produced exclusively for
WHSMITH

Reprinted 1979

ISBN 0 7063 4110 4

Produced specially for W.H. Smith & Sons by Ward Lock Ltd, 116 Baker Street, London W1M 2BB, a member of the Pentos Group.

Text filmset in Baskerville by Servis Filmsetting Ltd, Manchester

Printed and bound in Hong Kong by Leefung-Asco Printers Ltd.

Contents

Introduction

The hobby greenhouse in the back garden is everything you ever want to make it—productive, expensive, worrying, time-demanding, beautiful, but most of all it is a refuge! A refuge from what?—from everything that causes you annoyance (the wife for example?) from endless telly to the yapping dog. It is a refuge in very much the same way as the local, the golf-course or fishing are means of getting away from it for your neighbours. In spite of rising costs your pastime of growing plants in a greenhouse will be much less expensive than any of the hobbies mentioned above and, for the lover of plants, there really is nothing to compare with the pleasant atmosphere that prevails in the warm and humid greenhouse, especially on a cold winter's day.

As I have spent thirty years in the business of growing plants for my living, and a good many years caring for the contents of the 12ft by 8ft (3·6m × 2·4m) greenhouse in the back garden, the reader will find that this book evolves around the two approaches to growing the best possible plants. The reader will find, for example, that there are few references to ideal temperatures of say, 50°F (10°C) for fuchsias, because the author knows only too well that maintaining exact temperatures in the small house is almost impossible. You will also notice that the book is not a catalogued ABC list of plants with what one should or should not do with each one in order to be successful—if you want such a list, then save yourself the cost of a book and send for a free catalogue! In some respects you may find more plant names in the catalogue than within the pages of the book, and there may be glaring omissions in respect of some plants. But the management and care of greenhouses large and small is not so much about lists of names, it is more about getting one's jacket off and doing—and doing things in the right way.

The first piece of advice to someone with a new greenhouse is to suggest that there should be no hurry whatsoever in stocking it with plants. Although the interior may seem a vast void, you can take it from me that in a very short space of time you will be standing in the middle of the greenhouse with a plant in each hand wondering where on earth you are going to put the blessed things. And the man with a new, shiny and empty greenhouse is ever the target for the man with an established house that is filled with large, ugly and bug-ridden plants for which he is seeking a home. The policy should be to refuse all gifts at the outset and to be very selective about what you accept or puchase—one plant infested with red spider or mealy bug could well mean the new

A greenhouse creates its own mini-climate for tender plants

Every inch of space can be put to good use by using hanging baskets – this begonia is an especially good subject

greenhouse being filled with pests almost before the business of growing has got under way. You will also find that growing on your own healthy young plants will give infinitely more satisfaction than caring for someone else's cast-off plants that are long past their best.

The suggestion that someone may have greenfingers is often sneered at but, you know, even in the professional field there are those among us who are approvingly referred to as good growers. The professional good grower would look upon you with more than a little pity if you suggested that he had greenfingers, but the only difference is in the words used as they simply mean that there are folk about who have a way with plants, a better understanding of their needs than most of us with the result that plants seem to do better for them. My boss of many years is one of those good growers with a nose for trouble, and an ability to see the signs of impending problems long before they materialize as disasters. This is a quality that you cannot be taught—it is something that, if you are lucky, you learn over the years and put to good use.

Although the opposite would seem to be the case in some greenhouses, there are few plants that actually want to die, the majority are killed off for one reason or another! And a major reason for plant failure in the greenhouse can very often be traced to the compost in which the plant is growing. For survival the plant is almost totally dependent on the mixture that finds its way into the pot and around the roots, so it is essential that some care is exercised when mixing or purchasing. The magic name of John Innes potting mix is used frequently throughout this book, but the author has in mind top quality compost made from the proper ingredients and not a sackful of badly mixed clay and gravel that may have been lying around for months or even years prior to purchase. Get prepared compost from a known reliable source, or enjoy the pleasure of carefully mixing your own and seeing how well your plants respond to that little extra effort on their behalf.

Even the tiniest garden can have a mini-greenhouse

I often wonder why greenhouses are purchased in the first place, and what happens to the many millions that are dotted about in very average back gardens—some to flourish and others to become little more than bicycle stores. Whatever the reasons may be it should be realised that caring for a greenhouse takes time, and is almost equivalent to keeping chickens—you just cannot walk away and leave it; the chickens need feeding, and the greenhouse needs watering and a dozen other jobs throughout the year. And this is one reason why, when you start in the greenhouse business, you should purchase a small one just to see how you get on with it. There will always be time to expand when the great pleasure of growing nice things has really taken a hold.

A well-kept cedarwood greenhouse always looks attractive

1
The Greenhouse

My first greenhouse was constructed from old commercial greenhouse bars, running purlings, end rails and such like—needless to say it was a very much more laborious exercise than one would be expected to be confronted with now when contemplating the erection of a greenhouse. With second-hand material everything had to be cut, trimmed and somehow made to fit the chosen size of the house, whereas the modern greenhouse comes in a neat package with explicit and easily followed instructions for putting it together.

We hear many arguments for and against this and that type of greenhouse, and the various merits of each particular design. You can go through endless glossy catalogues in an effort to decide on the type of greenhouse that will be best suited to your needs, and the site you have, but it will be very much better for the would-be purchaser to take him or herself along to one or more of the many garden centres where a complete selection of greenhouses will be on display. Most greenhouses on show will be of metal construction, some will be in cedar wood, but there will be very few of the older style white painted timber houses. This is not to say that there will not be timber houses available for those who can afford the cost of upkeep—and there are still the specialist manufacturers about who will construct a timber greenhouse or conservatory to almost any shape that you may have in mind, circular or hexagonal shapes being quite within their scope.

Provided one has the time to maintain a timber greenhouse, especially with regard to regular painting, then it could well be the best choice, as almost any type of plant will look better for the fact that it is growing in a brightly painted timber greenhouse rather than in a grey aluminium framed house. Cedarwood greenhouses do not need painting in the conventional sense, but they will be much improved by regular treatment with teak oil.

Design

The commercial growers of glasshouse products, who depend for their living from their efforts, almost invariably employ span-roof type greenhouses to accommodate their plants. This could well be a guide for the amateur grower who is contemplating the purchase of a greenhouse. Span-roof houses may vary in height, or in width depending on the crop that is to be grown, or the pitch of the roof may vary, but in most respects they will be very similar. The cedar-framed Dutch light greenhouse offers a span-roof with a slight variation in that the sides of the greenhouse are gently sloping, but otherwise there is very little difference in the interior capacity of the house when compared to the more conventional structure.

The lean-to greenhouse is positioned against a supporting wall, the dwelling-house for example, but is not so very different from the span-roof house if you think of it as simply half of the latter with the dwelling-house being utilized as a supporting wall. Where space is limited the lean-to house is often the most sensible answer, and there will be the added advantage that when it is placed against the warm wall of a house, the interior will be that little bit warmer and the wall will be ideal for growing many fine climbing greenhouse plants against.

When deciding on a greenhouse, give particular attention to the solidity of the structure, and in particular to the way in which doors and ventilators are fitted. Badly fitting doors and vents are an indication of poor workmanship throughout, and will inevitably result in costly heat loss. Be sure too that the house is fitted with guttering and down-pipes, as there is nothing worse than rain water being shed from the roof of the greenhouse and in time making a muddy mess all round. Furthermore, rain water collected in a water butt will be a very useful commodity once the business of growing plants in the greenhouse begins—particularly so if the house and source of water is some distance away.

Ventilation and light

Although you must be ever mindful of the high cost involved in heating a greenhouse this should not blind you to the need for purchasing a house that is adequately provided with ventilators. Costly and problematical it may be at times during the winter months to keep the greenhouse adequately heated, but it will be an equally difficult problem during the warmer months of the year to keep the temperature down to a reasonable level. This makes it necessary to have reasonably large ventilators on both sides of the roof of the greenhouse and in the side walls also if the growing plants require maximum circulation of air. The door of the house can also be brought into play to aid air circulation on very hot days, but this may mean fixing a secondary door made of chicken wire if the neighbourhood cats are to be discouraged from using the house as a warm and comfortable retreat!

The glass of the greenhouse should be clear and the more slender the supporting structure then the more light will be available to the plants within the house, and adequate light is almost the most important requirement of the majority of plants that one will contemplate growing. The metal framed greenhouse scores in this respect, as it offers rigidity and strength, yet using comparatively slim glazing bars and supports.

Choosing a site

Selecting and preparing the site for the greenhouse is often put forward as a matter for deep concern and contemplation, but my experience suggests that very few gardeners have much choice, as the size and shape of the garden dictate where the

A half-wall cedarwood greenhouse

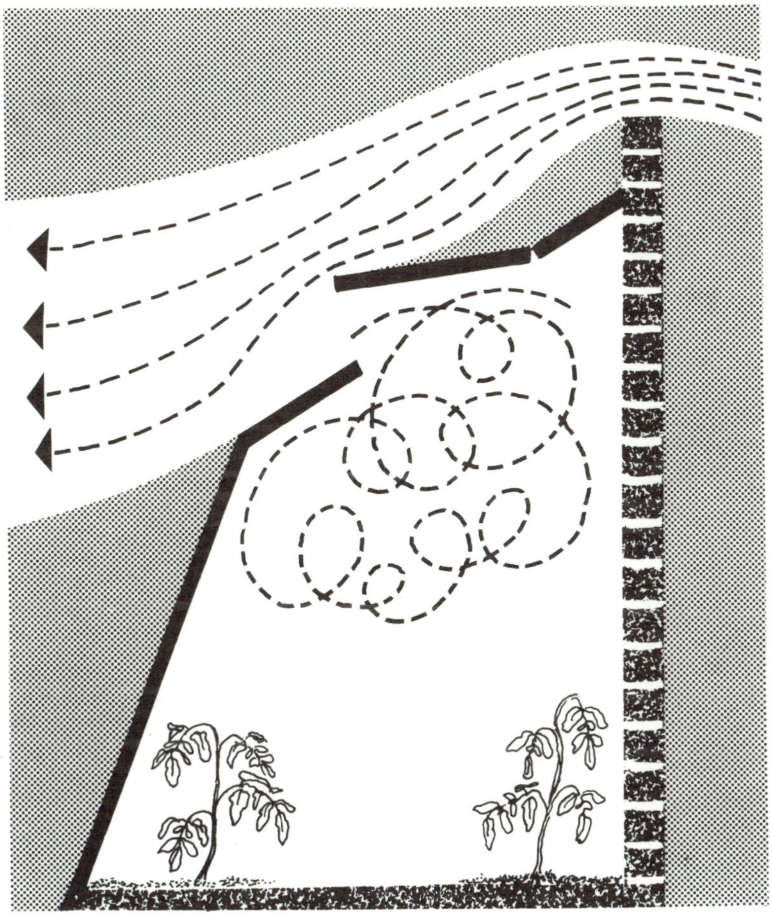

It is important to see that a lean-to receives sufficient ventilation

greenhouse will be located. But supposing you are fortunate enough to be able to say that the house can be located in all manner of different positions. You may then listen to the pundits as they tell you that the ideal orientation in respect of the sun is a north/south aspect, as the house will have an even amount of sunlight throughout daylight hours. Theoretically there would seem to be every reason for believing that a north/south orientation is ideal, but my experience suggests that, both commercially and for the amateur, it makes very little difference either way. The most important requirement to meet is that the house be located well away from the harmful shade of tall trees and buildings, as maximum light is an essential need of almost all greenhouse plants. Protection from northerly or prevailing winds should also be considered. This may well mean locating the greenhouse on the south facing side of a building, and this could well be the best position for a lean-to type house.

In any garden, large or small, the greenhouse should be a major attraction; it should offer colour and interest all the year round. So why is it that so many greenhouses are tucked away in some remote corner of the garden surrounded by sheds, compost heaps, broken bicycles and the like— often enough as the interest wanes the greenhouse also becomes a sort of shed for housing all manner of unwanted wreckage. Perhaps the choice of site

One of the latest concepts in greenhouses – the geodetic style

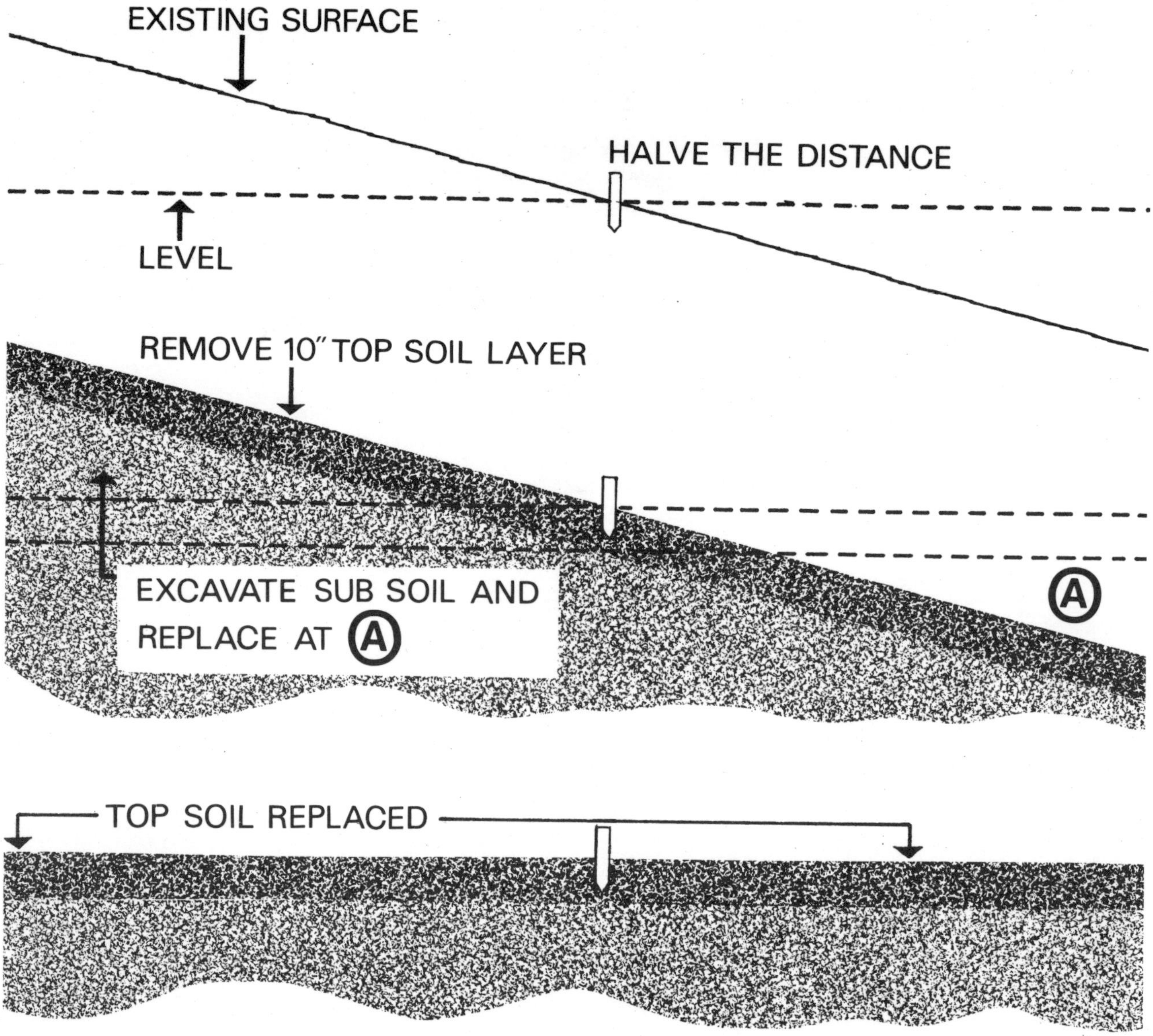

It is essential that the site should be level

amongst the rubbish of the garden is one very good reason for the would-be greenhouse enthusiast losing his, or her enthusiasm—after all, who wants to leave the warm fireside and trudge down to the least appealing part of the garden on a winter's night to see what the temperature is? And, if you are proud of your achievements in the greenhouse, then you will be keen to show it off to almost everyone who cares to call—and who is going to be courageous enough to step through the debris in the least interesting part of the garden?

If you once decide to have a greenhouse, it should be located not too far from the house and be made an important feature of the garden with a hard path leading up to the door. On an untidy site the most well-meaning gardener will in time tend to become untidy in his greenhouse—instead of cleaning and storing unused pots he will litter the surroundings of the greenhouse with them. And when you lose your pride in the job, then you are well on your way to turning the greenhouse into a cycle shed! On a prominent site the need for keeping the area surrounding the greenhouse clean will become every bit as important as the weekly mowing of the lawns. As a practical proposition and in the interests of keep-

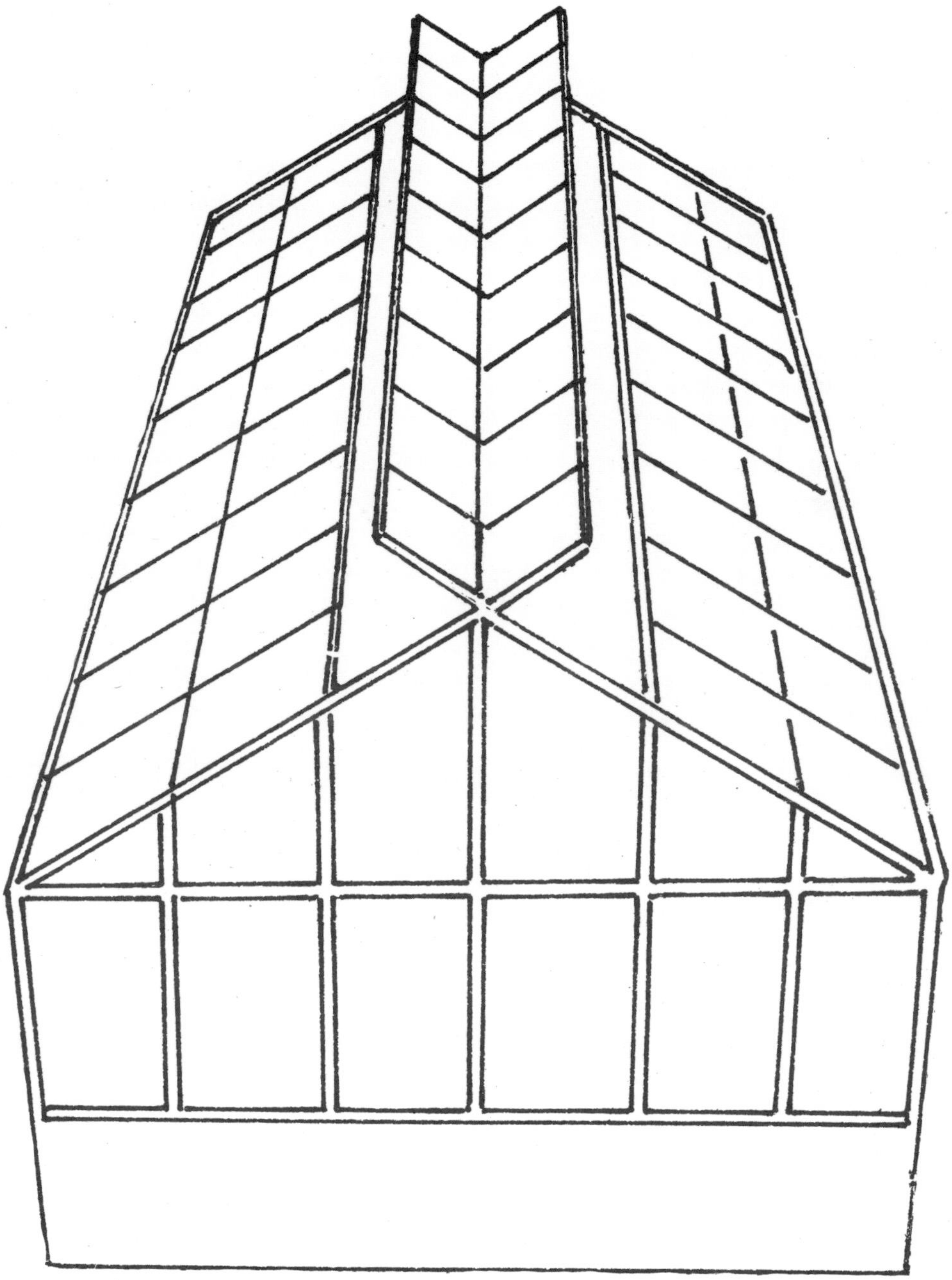

Continuous two-sided ventilation can be invaluable

ing up appearances it will be a considerable advantage to have a small shed built as a continuation of the greenhouse with a door leading from one to the other. All of the greenhouse area can then be used for growing plants and the shed used for storage and for carrying out many of the essential jobs such as potting.

Make the task of caring for the plants as pleasant as possible, so arrange for a weatherproof electric cable to be laid to the greenhouse so that the business of attending to your plants can go on into the night. 'If need be' was almost added to the last sentence, but anyone with a knowledge of greenhouses, however little, will realize that there is a continuous need to carry on with the many jobs that will demand your attention long after

It is generally possible to add an extension later to an aluminium greenhouse

the hours of daylight. (My wife has long since been convinced that her husband is possessed of some catlike ability that enables him to see in the dark when caring for his precious plants!) Consider a supply of electricity an essential need rather than a luxury item, as there are so many greenhouse aids that are totally dependent on a supply of power. There seem to be so many aids to growing that I wonder how long it will be before the grower of the plants is needed at all—soon the robot will walk up the garden path, deposit the cut carnations on the kitchen table, then return to finish off the watering!

A water tap inside or immediately outside the greenhouse will be a considerable asset and will ensure that plants are adequately watered, whereas there is always a tendency to skimp with the watering if a long trek with the watering can becomes necessary.

What size should the greenhouse be?

The greenhouse of the enthusiastic grower is always too small, there is never sufficient space to accommodate all the plants under his care to best advantage. As one's knowledge of plants improves, so the quality and size of the plants improves with the inevitable result that they require more space in which to grow. Every square inch of space is utilized; pots suspended on wires, temporary shelving, even the area beneath the staging. I mention these things so that those who can afford

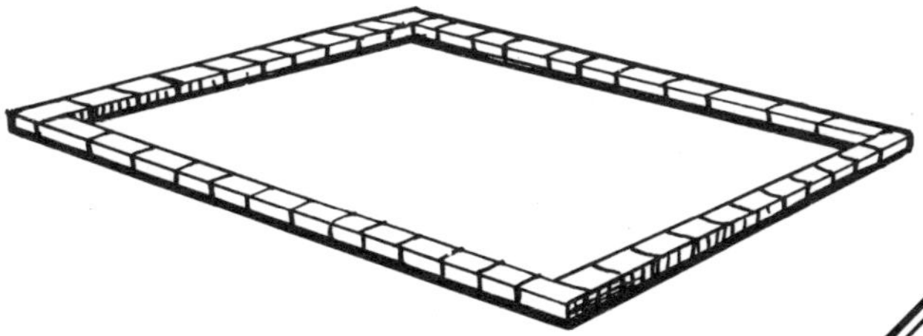

Above and overleaf: stages in the erection of a greenhouse – get a friend to help you

the extra cost may opt for the greenhouse that is just that little bit wider or that little bit longer, so that the interior does not become too cramped too quickly. It is also a good reason for the greenhouse purchaser to think in terms of the greenhouse that can be extended as his interest in growing plants increases. Most greenhouses can be simply extended by removing the back and inserting additional side and roof panels before refitting the rear section.

When erecting the greenhouse, give some thought to the possibility of providing two separate environments under the same roof by fitting either a glass, or thick clear polythene divider which will enable you to have a warm and a cool section in the same greenhouse. The warm section can be quite small, yet be capable of growing a wide range of plants at much smaller

cost than if the entire house were heated to temperatures in the region of 65°F (18°C). The insulating partition will require a door which can be simply made from a light wood framework to which the clear polythene is neatly pinned. When delivered the modern aluminium greenhouse is in a very neat package that takes up very little space, with the cut-to-size glass in a separate container, or containers. The timber greenhouse will be a little more bulky, but it will be in sections that simply require bolting together for the new owner to be in business. Some even come with their concrete foundations. But it is never as easy as it sounds, is it? The instructions for erection may say 'Dig out the foundations . . .'. Digging out the foundations may seem all very simple, but my experience suggests that that simple task can be fraught with problems. Almost everyone knows a builder or a handyman, and my advice is that he should be contacted and asked to lay the foundations, with perhaps the added luxury of a low brick wall to which the greenhouse can be bolted as a start to the erection performance. About this time it would also be wise to be on the best terms with the neighbours so that one, or preferably two, of them can be called upon to assist with the putting together of the new toy, as it will seem at the time!

Erecting the greenhouse

For the man who digs his own foundations, it is suggested that a trench be dug down to firm subsoil, and about 15in (38cm) wide. Fill the trench with concrete, mixed at four shovels of sand and gravel to one of cement, and check with a straight board and spirit level to ensure that the foundations are level. On an uneven site it will be necessary to have more depth of concrete on one side than the other, and this may mean using shuttering boards to bring up the level. (It really would be wise to consult the handyman, if only to get his advice on your particular site.) By accurately measuring the base width of the greenhouse coach bolts can be let into the concrete while it is still soft, with the threaded end of the bolts well above the surface of the concrete. If not already there holes can be drilled in the base plate of the greenhouse so that they coincide with the coach bolts—you can then screw the greenhouse firmly in position on its foundation.

While the concrete is being mixed and general upheaval reigns, it may also be a good time for

Circular greenhouses are unusual and attractive

laying a concrete path through the centre of the greenhouse. Other than the path one should avoid permanent fixtures in the greenhouse, as you will always be wanting to grow different types of plants, and generally to change the scene inside the house, and this will be difficult if you have to break up concrete floors, walls and the like. At all costs avoid concreting the floor all over as this will preclude the eventual possibility of growing plants in soil in the greenhouse. The concrete path need not be too wide, but it should be wide enough for the edges of the path to act as a foundation for supports that will hold up the staging which will probably be installed. Although it is important to have a clean, hard footing inside the greenhouse that can be washed down and help improve the interior of the house, it is also worth considering having a similarly clean appearance outside. But, rather than lay permanent concrete paths around the outside of the house, it is better to lay slabs which can be more easily removed should the occasion arise. When slabbing the outside area it is worth considering the possibility that cold frames will become an important part of the greenhouse scene: it could be good sense to leave a stretch about 3ft (90cm) in width between the greenhouse and the path on either side.

Types of greenhouse

It is not easy to say which type of greenhouse to purchase if it is the very first house that someone has ever had, as all the houses have their merits and much depends on the sort of plants that one intends to grow. In fact, the total beginner could well be advised simply to purchase a small greenhouse to experiment with and just be sure that caring for such a demanding animal really is their scene. If it is not, then the cost of the smaller greenhouse will not have been such a costly experiment. Alternatively, having succeeded with the smaller house you can then consider something more elaborate—the experience gained from it will be very valuable when it comes to investing in something a little grander.

If you want to grow potted plants to present a permanent display, then the timber greenhouse with straight sides could well be the most satisfactory acquisition. If the lower half of the side wall is wood rather than glass this will be all the better as far as insulation is concerned. For a wood-sided house of this sort, before putting in the staging, soak the inside thoroughly with wood preservative as it will surely be a long time before you pluck up the courage to remove the staging in order to treat the timber. Also, after treating the wood it is worthwhile double-lining the area under the bench and packing the space between outer and inner walls with fibre glass insulating material. It is essential to make a good job of lining the inside if the insulating material is not to become a home for all the spiders and unwanted beasties in the neighbourhood.

If growing tomatoes or cucumbers to be followed by late chrysanthemums is your intention then it will be necessary to purchase a house that is glazed down to floor level, so that maximum light is available to the plants.

Besides all the other factors give some consideration to the greenhouse that offers reasonable height, because when you really get under way there will be plants everywhere and there is no pleasure to be had from knocking your head on suspended pots and hanging baskets every time you enter your tropical retreat. As to what size is most suitable—the short answer to that is that you should get the largest house you can afford and manage with reasonable competence. You will find as time goes on that there is never enough space for all the plants that you acquire, and it is never very long before you are standing with a pot in each hand wondering where in heaven's name you are going to place them.

2 Equipping the Greenhouse

An Aladdin paraffin heater

After a lifetime of growing plants, both commercially and purely for pleasure, there is still for me a glow of appreciation when I enter a greenhouse full of plants that is warm and has some 'feeling' to it. Feeling in a greenhouse is an undefineable quality, but it is that mixture of humidity and warmth that tells the experienced grower of plants that all is well—and if the grower approves, then you can rest assured that the plants also approve of the conditions that prevail. Not everyone can afford the heating bills that are necessary to provide an ideal amount of feeling for more tender plants, and not all plants are happy in the greenhouse that is too warm and humid for their needs. However, if the greenhouse is to become a worthwhile hobby and the owner is to get the maximum benefit from his efforts, then heating of some kind or other must be provided.

When it comes to choosing the most appropriate type of heating we all have our likes and dislikes, and the majority are controlled by what can be afforded. However, one can obtain surprisingly good results from paraffin heaters, the cheapest of all, provided the apparatus is kept clean and top quality fuel is used.

My first experience of heating a small greenhouse was of using a solid fuel boiler through 4in (10cm) heating pipes filled with water and an expansion tank at one end. And if you have the time that is required to tend to its ever-demanding needs, then this could well be the best way of heating your greenhouse—it will also be reasonably economical. However, be warned that a solid fuel boiler is a demanding animal in that it will need regular attention, both in respect of cleaning and filling with fuel at night to ensure that there are no disasters in the morning. Solid fuel boilers

A fan heater (courtesy of Humex)

A tubular heater (courtesy of Humex)

can be adapted to operate on oil, or an oil fired boiler can be fitted—with a thermostat to control the temperature it will be much less demanding of time. It is a little more costly to operate, however, but one should expect to pay a little more for the time that is saved.

Heating by electricity, whether it be tubular wall-mounted heaters or an air-warming fan heater, will be more expensive. However, the convenience factor here reaches the point whereby very little attention is required other than paying the bill when the demand appears on the breakfast table! The fan heater tends to dry the atmosphere which is a disadvantage, but to compensate the fan may be used to circulate fresh air when the greenhouse becomes excessively hot during the summer months.

When installing electrical apparatus in the greenhouse, seek the advice, probably more sensibly the services, of a competent electrician who will instal the moisture-proof fittings that are so essential where there is so much water about. All electrical fittings should be mounted well off the ground, and out of the way of hose pipes and watering cans.

Heaters operating on North Sea gas or natural gas will also be more costly to instal, but there should be no fears about the efficiency of natural gas heaters which, besides heating the greenhouse, also enrich the atmosphere with carbon dioxide which will improve plant growth.

An air circulator causes the continual movement of air which is necessary in a greenhouse for healthy plant growth (courtesy of Humex)

Simplest of all will be the paraffin heater, as it is easy to fit and the running costs are comparatively low. For the beginner, until he or she gets more experienced with the management of the greenhouse, the paraffin heater is probably the most sensible purchase. Almost every aspect of greenhouse management is discovered by trial and error, whether it relates to heating or plant growing, and everyone learns by early mistakes. And as one's interest develops, so one comes into contact with more and more greenhouse owners, possibly at the local horticultural club, and when you mix with the enthusiastic greenhouse owning community then there will be no shortage of advice on every aspect of heating the greenhouse and caring for the plants within. It would be foolish to accept all the advice that is offered, but that is not to say that you should not listen to it all and glean from it what you feel will be to your advantage.

An automatic ventilator can save a lot of work

Ventilation

The heating of the greenhouse will probably be the most expensive item, but, as mentioned earlier, it should not blind you to the fact that keeping the greenhouse cool during the hot summer months can be an equally difficult proposition. Therefore it is important that the house should be adequately provided with means of ventilation, with ventilators opening along the ridge of the greenhouse and along the sides if it is practical. Conventional ventilators are important, but it should be remembered that the largest ventilator in the house will be the door—when fully opened the door will admit much more fresh air than all the vents put together. We could go back at this point to the positioning of the greenhouse and suggest that when the house is located in the garden some consideration should be given to

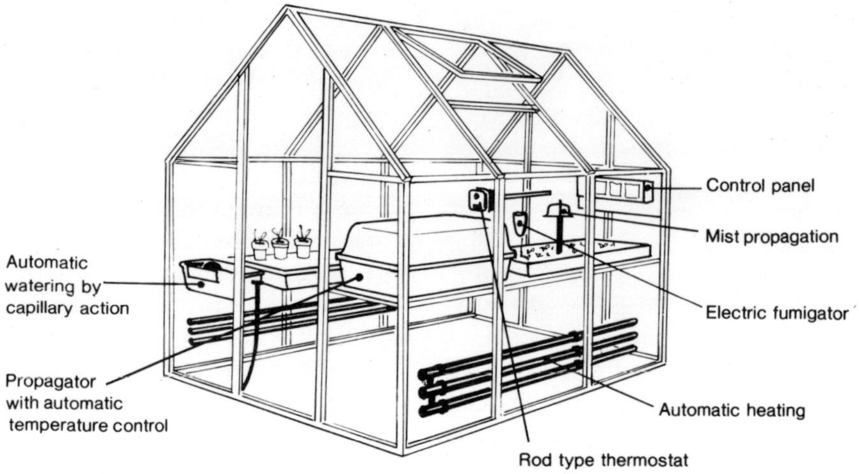

A diagram showing all possible kinds of automation for the greenhouse

prevailing or northerly wind aspects, and to ensure that the door is on the lee or south side of the building. If you do this, the door can be opened on cooler days without causing too much drop in temperature inside, and it will also enable you to slip in and out on colder days without the accompanying icy blast that would be present if the door was northerly orientated.

At a commercial establishment airing the greenhouses when the sun unexpectedly appears is a simple matter as there is always someone on hand to attend to it, but for the solitary greenhouse in the back garden it can be a very different matter. Its protector and general nursemaid may have caught the 7·45 to town when the day was very cold and may not even know that the precious contents of his glass sanctuary are being baked out of their minds by midday. It is then that the one who stays at home, be it wife or husband, comes into their own—if they have been properly trained they will immediately note that the sun has come out, the temperature risen, and that it is time the greenhouse was aired. Of course, with really proper training, the one left in the house would also automatically pick up the water can on entering the very warm greenhouse—not to water the plants (you could hardly trust them with that!), but to damp down the path and under the staging so that some of that 'feeling' spoken of earlier could be introduced! You haven't got anyone at home to open the vents in your absence?—then you will have to invest in a simple piece of mechanism that will open and close the vents automatically in your absence when the temperature reaches a pre-set level. Names of suppliers will be found in almost every gardening magazine and the supplier will be delighted to send you all the most up-to-date information on all his many mechanical aids to greenhouse management, and you can then make your choice from there. In fact, for someone like myself who was brought up on very rudimentary greenhouse mechanical aids (like a ventilator lever on the end of the greenhouse that lifted thirty or so vents at one time!) the increasing number of labour saving devices becomes ever more bewildering. At a garden centre recently the owner showed me his small display greenhouse that was fitted with all the labour saving items

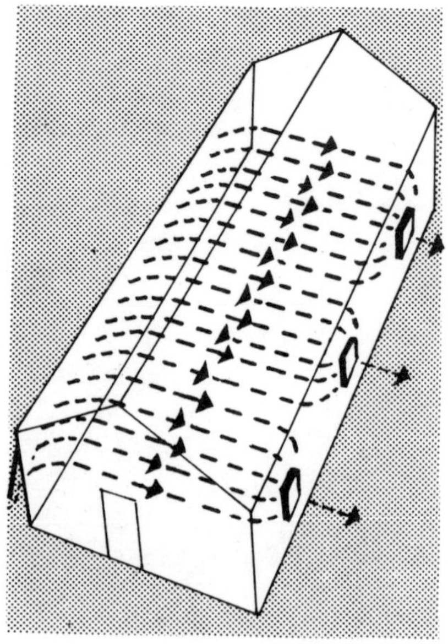

Air flow with fan ventilation

Roller blinds

that the country's leading manufacturer could provide. The man was amazed when his guest did not register immediate enthusiasm for his wonder of the age—alas, to me it had more the appearance of an operating theatre than a greenhouse. Have devices like vent openers, propagating cases, capillary watering and thermostatically controlled heating by all means, but do remember that it is a hobby after all, and that at least half the pleasure of owning a greenhouse is not in admiring the plants, it is in doing things for them. Doing things like watering, cleaning, potting, damping down and opening that vent just that fraction more as you yourself feel that it is necessary—you've got to be master of your own household, sorry greenhouse, after all.

Shading

Possibly one of the most neglected sides of growing plants in a greenhouse is shading—not all plants need to be shaded from the sun, but it is most essential that those that do should be protected. The old fashioned method of applying shading to the glass on the outside of the greenhouse is trouble-free, relatively cheap and effective. Care must be taken to avoid a blanket effect that will exclude beneficial light as well as the sun, but it is important that sufficient shading be applied to prevent plants becoming scorched and hardened by the sun's rays. Roller blinds can be fitted, but this will require the services of the one left at home who can adjust the blinds as weather conditions demand—blinds left permanently in position will restrict the amount of light and be detrimental to many plants. More untidy and more troublesome is rush matting which can be placed on the glass on the outside of the greenhouse. A shaded house will be much more pleasant to work in, and if it is more pleasant for you then you can rest assured that the plants will also be better pleased with the conditions.

Equipping the greenhouse can be a costly and almost unending task, but there really is no need to go out and purchase a greenhouse plus all the possible equipment in the same way as you would when purchasing a motor car. The motor car will only function effectively when all the parts are present (sometimes not even then!), but the ancillary gear for the greenhouse can be acquired as you go along and acquire more knowledge concerning what is useful and what is a luxury. However, there are fundamental items that you must have if anything is to be done at all, but these need not be extensive—a watering can with fine and coarse roses, a thermometer that will register maximum and minimum recordings and a fine syringe that can be used for spraying water onto the foliage or for applying liquid insecticides. Other than those, possibly a bucket for mixing feed and insecticides and if you really want to go the full hog possibly a brick to hold the door open.

Staging

If it is your intention to grow roses, tomatoes, lettuces or other plants which will stand on the floor of the greenhouse then there is very little need to do anything with the interior of the house. But if you are growing conventional pot plants, cacti, alpines or any smaller items in pots or boxes, then it is essential that some form of staging be erected for placing the plants on. Sure, they could be placed directly onto the floor of the house, but plants standing on the cold floor of a greenhouse seldom do very well—if there is no possibility of having staging then the plants should be placed on upturned pots or boxes so that there is some circulation of warm air between the pot and the cold floor of the house. When constructing staging you should start as you mean to go on and to make the best possible job of it. Once you have got under

A general view of a well-managed greenhouse

Trickle system on a wire mesh bench

way by using broken boxes and old five-gallon drums to support the staging then that is how it seems to go on, but by setting a higher standard in the beginning you seem able to take much more pride in the entire operation. For staging use stout supports of either timber or metal and treat them thoroughly with an appropriate preservative before the sections are fixed in position. Strong cross members can then be used to form the table part of the staging, and if possible acquire strong asbestos corrugated sheets for placing on the tabling. On the asbestos place a 2in (5cm) layer of a moisture-retaining material such as sand, peat, washed gravel or Leca pebbles and level it out. Fix white painted 3 × 1in (8 × 2·5cm) edging along the front of the staging to keep the covering material in position and you will be in business. The width between the staging, the path, is not important, but bear in mind that the wider the path is the fewer plants you will be able to accommodate.

For the busy person with little time it would be well worth investigating the possibility of installing capillary watering benches. In this event the staging must again be strongly made and flat sheets of asbestos used instead of corrugated ones, and it will be of paramount importance to ensure that the surface of the bench is level front to back and end to end. The bench is covered with thick gauge polythene with an overlap at sides and ends. Timber 3 × 1in (8 × 2·5cm) is then fixed round the polythene to act as a retaining wall, and sand is filled into the polythene tray and levelled off up to the height of the surrounding timber. The sand is then thoroughly saturated before placing plants on it to draw water up by capillary action as it is required. There are a number of devices on the market which can be fitted to ensure an even and continuous supply of water to the capillary bed. Plastic pots that are thin at the base and amply provided with drainage holes are more suitable than clay pots for capillary watering.

Many of the flowering pot plants prefer to grow on slatted staging which will ensure the maximum amount of air circulation around the plants, but it will be much more difficult to maintain them as they will need more frequent watering than those on a non-slatted surface.

You may feel that other essentials have been missed out—things like pots, compost, dibbers, seed boxes, crocks, cobwebs and sundry items, but these belong to the shed at the back of the greenhouse and not to the place where you are to grow your super things for the neighbours and all and sundry to come and admire. The suggestion has just been made that the edging to the staging should be painted white, and this may seem a trifle alien to the mucky business of growing things in a greenhouse. But very often it is only as mucky as you make it—if you paint the front of the staging white and keep it white you take a pride in what you are doing. And by putting all the bits and pieces in the shed where they should be you resist the temptation to establish a bug-infested paradise of rubbish under the staging. Put gravel under the staging and rake it over once in a while and you will be amazed at the difference it will make to the overall appearance of the place. Rubbish and pots attract more rubbish and pots, so make every effort to square things up and put them away when you have done with them.

Lighting

A final piece of equipment for the greenhouse should be a light over your head with which you can see to work on those darker evenings when you have had more than your fill of watching television repeat programmes. The neighbours may initially wonder what strange person it is who inhabitates the greenhouse when he could be transfixed by that great modern wonder the telly—but they don't know that what's going on in the greenhouse might result in an equally great wonder in the following summer when winter efforts mature into summer blooms!

3 How Plants Grow in the Greenhouse

The exotic plant trapped in its heated greenhouse is, by definition, in a very artificial stituation. Not only that, it is also totally at the tender, or otherwise, mercy of the man in charge and the amount of heat that can be produced by the boiler in order to maintain an agreeable temperature. Some would have us believe that all the plants would be better off if they were returned to their little niche in the Caribbean, or wherever. But this need not be so, and the perfect example of plants looking very much the better for enjoying the controlled conditions prevailing in the modern greenhouse is the poinsettia, *Euphorbia pulcherrima*, which is equally attractive as a compact pot plant as it is as an untidy shrub in its native habitat.

To grow at all in the greenhouse plants need light, air, moisture, adequate warmth and some form of nourishment to stimulate growth. And all these need to be given at the correct level as too much or too little of any will at least be harmful, if not fatal, to the plant. Some plants, such as *sansevieria*, will tolerate extremes of conditions much more successfully than others, but even the *sansevieria* will turn up its toes and die if the growing mix is permanently saturated or if the temperature drops and remains below 45°F (7°C) for any length of time. It will almost certainly die should the conditions remain cold and wet for even a comparatively short space of time. Over the years generations of greenhouse gardeners in the commercial and the amateur field have grown plants of almost every description and learned to know the likes and dislikes of most of them. But you will meet few men in the glasshouse business who are prepared to have themselves described as 'experts' —they probably, rather most certainly, know that plants in pots in greenhouses are fickle things: you may well have an excellent crop one year, do exactly the same thing with the crop the following year, only to find that the results are disastrous. You can never become complacent about growing plants in greenhouses, there is always a new challenge and new problem to be met and one supposes that this is one good reason for taking a deal of pride in the job when it is well done. For the beginner it is unwise to be too ambitious with the first greenhouse—in the first year or two it is much more sensible to experiment and get the feel of growing easy or simple plants before attempting more difficult subjects. Generally speaking, the more difficult the plant, codiaeums for example, then the higher the temperature it will require in order to succeed. This may mean making a start with an unheated, or cold house in which one can grow a reasonably interesting range of plants, tomatoes planted in late April, strawberries for an early crop, hardy winter lettuce, even grapes above your head. Camellias, one of the most beautiful of garden flowers, do particu-

Trickle lines

Mixed coleus add plenty of colour to the greenhouse scene

larly well in the unheated greenhouse if it is well ventilated. Later in the year when summer warmth is about it will be possible to grow all manner of colourful and interesting plants in pots and hanging baskets—fuchsias, tuberous begonias, calceolarias, streptocarpus, schizanthus; all sorts of beautiful things, really. The difficulty is, though, that none of these could be successfully overwintered in the cold greenhouse and fresh young plants would have to be purchased annually. This may seem to defeat the purpose of having a greenhouse which suggests that you should do everything for yourself, sow the seed, mix the growing medium and so on. But if you have no heat in the house then you have no alternative, and to stock a small greenhouse with young plants in late spring is not a costly business. The professional raises the plants for you in his heated greenhouses and you pay him for that service by purchasing his plants. And there are always plenty of fine quality young plants about for you to pick from—you can choose from a host of lovely things, put them into slightly larger pots when you get them home and have a very fine display that is well ahead of similar plants that you may have raised from seed sown much later than those in the heated greenhouse.

Heating levels

In the early spring when it can be quite cold during the night it is important to water plants

A propagating case showing soil-warming cables (courtesy of Humex)

sparingly, and for preference to do any watering that is necessary early in the day as it will be harmful to plants to lie wet and cold overnight. The temperature of the cold house can be lifted a few degrees by lining the entire inside of the house with thin gauge clear polythene, but condensation dripping from the polythene can be harmful to any plants that may be in flower. Alternatively, if it is a small house you could put the thing to bed on very cold nights by covering the entire greenhouse in a polythene wrap. Daft you may think, but this we did with a low, 60ft (18m) house in the winter of '63/64 and raised the temperature inside the house by 10°F (6°C), which was enough to save the plants. Climbing onto the ridge to do the job is not recommended, but it should be little trouble to envelope an average size house in a polythene shroud, and save the plants. This is a tip that may also help with the warm greenhouse when the heating plays up and plants are in peril.

From the unheated greenhouse the next most natural step is to the cool house which maintains a minimum temperature of not less than 40°F (4°C)—this, however, does not mean that the house is permanently at 40°, it will be somewhat higher most of the time and at this level when the temperature is low outside. When you maintain this sort of house you can really begin to feel that you are in the business of growing more interesting plants than your neighbour can manage on her window sill. It is a kind of refuge on colder days, and a house where endless hours will be spent attending to all manner of interesting plants—yet you will never reach the point where you can stand back and feel that there is nothing more to be done.

You can now grow all sorts of interesting and colourful plants, particularly in the flowering line—zonal pelargoniums, primulas, better fuchsias than in a coldhouse, cinerarias, perpetual flowering carnations, and you could have a go with spring sown cyclamen that will flower in about eight or nine months and be ready for early December. With the cool house you have to be especially careful with watering during the winter and early spring when temperatures drop and, because of heat loss there is a reluctance to air the house. Dank conditions that are a perfect breeding ground for fungus troubles will be the result, and these conditions can create havoc with all manner of plants. Dank conditions also result where plants are crowded too close together preventing free circulation of air. Plants that are packed in very tightly may seem to give more value to your efforts as there are so many more plants, but this is a lot of baloney. It is far better to grow one good plant than it is to grow half a dozen in the same space if few or none of them will be any good. Each plant should have its own space on the staging, and not be crushed up against its neighbours so that they all deteriorate—if the plant is getting too large for its allotted space then it is time to get rid of it, give it to the man down the road with a new greenhouse to fill(!), or sell it to the local flower shop. Alternatively, you could make a wire hanger to fix around the rim of the pot and hang it above your head where there is usually more than enough room to spare; remember the point made earlier about having a greenhouse with reasonable height!

The warm greenhouse is where it all happens, where you can grow almost anything in addition to the cool house subjects if you have a reasonable amount of skill to help the plants along the sometimes rough road to maturity. The minimum temperature here is in the region of 55°F (12°C) and, depending on the heating system you have installed it may be getting on for double the cost to maintain this temperature compared to the cool greenhouse. How do you overcome this—perhaps you could stop smoking, or persuade yourself that it is no more costly than your nieghbour's tobacco bill. Or you could follow my example of earlier years with my first greenhouse and sell some of the plants when they are mature. A bit mercenary, you may feel, to try to make money from what is ostensibly your hobby. Not a bit of it, the best thing for any greenhouse crop regardless of where it may have been grown is to get rid of the plants when they are at their best, either by selling them or donating them to the many worthy causes that exist in every locality.

Do not let your plants outgrow you

The principal reason for the commercial man appearing to do things so much better than the majority of amateur growers is that when his crop matures he disposes of it. Whereas the amateur is more inclined to hang on to the dear things that he has nurtured and cared for over the years (sometimes years and years and years!), when it would be much more preferable to take a few cuttings or whatever from the old faithful and to grow one or two healthy and vigorous young plants to replace it.

Really, the field is wide open when you own a warm greenhouse, you can enter the exotic but not to difficult field of orchid growing, have your own poinsettias for Christmas (with luck), grow tropical codiaeums and bougainvilleas, or tender ferns, or fill the house with cucumber plants. A happy thought, and the really ambitious person may feel that they can manage all these things

A terrarium can be heated quite cheaply within the greenhouse

Cucumbers growing in the greenhouse

Pleome reflexa – a difficult greenhouse subject, but rewarding

under one roof, in the same temperature and with the same amount of shading—but you would be setting off on a very difficult passage if you were to attempt to grow all these wondrous things in the same environment. Whatever else you may in time discover about growing plants in the greenhouse there is one clear message which you can have at this very moment without going through the aggravation of finding out for yourself. And that is that the most difficult crop to grow under one greenhouse roof is a mixed one, the greater the mixture then the greater the difficulty. Codiaeums, poinsettias and sansevierias require full light in order to succeed, whereas ferns and marantas are much happier in heavily shaded conditions. The codiaeum and fern will need abundant moisture during the entire year, whereas the sansevieria will do perfectly well on practically no moisture—so you see that it is a complicated permutation of setting one problem against another and trying to come up with a satisfactory blend.

One has seen so many pathetically sad small greenhouses filled with the most incredible assortment of bug-ridden rubbishy plants that are totally unsuited to the conditions that prevail, there comes a time when you feel it would be kinder, rather than offer advice, to tell the owner to give up. Happily there is a solution to the problem, and that is that as the greenhouse owner develops his interest there is a tendency to gravitate towards one type of plant—to become a specialist if you like. He may grow a few other plants, but his main interest will centre around chrysanthemums (or these and tomatoes as a combined interest), fuchsias, pelargoniums, orchids, ferns, cacti, alpines or assorted foliage plants requiring similar treatment. There are specialist societies that continually foster interest in their particular type of plant, perhaps a local one in your own town, and they are well worth getting in touch with—if only to give you the opportunity to exhibit your plants at their shows.

This chapter is called How Plants Grow in the Greenhouse, and I could offer all sorts of advice on the way plants grow in greenhouses—depending on the treatment and the prevailing conditions. But it can be said that plants with their roots confined to pots will grow more slowly than the same plant freely planted in the soil on the floor of the house. Another tip, here: avoid the temptation to free plant such things as hoyas and stephanotis, as the lush growth that usually develops will be totally unsuited to the confines of a small greenhouse. They also become ridden with mealy bug and all the other pests that are seeking a warm, comfortable and comparatively undisturbed home. Having permanent plants clambering around the upper reaches of the house supported by string, tape and the lord knows what else will make the annual spring clean and scrub down of the interior of the house very difficult. Whereas in pots, though growth may be less vigorous, one can take the pot out of doors and set to with the scrubbing brush and Jeyes Fluid to brighten the scene for the ensuing season.

If you have a gas heater, make sure it has an adequate flue so that the air is not poisoned for the plants

Greenhouse hygiene

Which leads us on to hygiene in the greenhouse—keep it clean at all costs, an annual coat of paint works wonders for the timber house and an annual clean out of gathering moss, cobwebs and the like will improve the look of the metal house. Mention has already been made of keeping the area underneath the staging free of clutter—avoid the temptation to put empty pots there, and do this by putting a row of plants that will tolerate limited light along the path and just under the staging. Place them on upturned pots and this will prevent leaves that would otherwise be touching the ground being damaged. You'll be amazed by the number of plants that you can get into the small greenhouse if you study all the possibilities—for example, you can grow half standard fuchsias and space them out between the other pots on the staging. It will not crowd the lower plants as there are no leaves on the lower part of the fuchsia and it will add another dimension to the overall scene. Getting back to hygiene, one feels that it should go without saying that dead leaves should be conveyed to the compost heap as they appear, but it does need mentioning as so many leaves are left on the plant and on the staging to collect all the diseases and pests that are going. Remember, dead leaves do nothing for a plant other than mar its appearance, so have them off and into the bin. A simple suggestion but it will help plants to grow in the greenhouse.

Preparing a seedbox – line box with coarse peat and cover with growing compost. After placing seeds cover to right depth and firm with flat piece of wood

What the plants grow in

Next to adequate temperature and correct light the next most important need for plants that are growing in a greenhouse is a compost that is suited to the plant's particular needs. We frequently hear folk talk of potting their plants into garden dirt—to my mind, dirt coming from the average garden and put in a pot would be almost certain death to the vast majority of plants. The bother with garden dirt is that it is something of an unknown commodity and will almost surely be lacking in the nutrient value that is essential to plants when their roots are confined to a comparatively small amount of soil. It will also be badly drained, which is a further disadvantage.

We still have old boys at the nursery who can bring out their little black (can't think why they are all black!) notebooks showing exactly the right medium for every potted plant that was ever grown on the place; also the dates of planting

Peat pots with phlox and marigold seedlings

cucumbers and tomatoes in the greenhouses are carefully recorded. Almost every potted plant had its own special mixture, and it would seem that weathered soot featured in most of them! In the mid-30s, the John Innes potting composts, after much experiment, became available, and many of the little black books were put to one side as these general purpose mixes were used. But it is only fair to add that many of the old potting mix recipes are still used for some plants, and the secret of the concoction is still jealously guarded.

Although you can mix your own J.I. it becomes a somewhat tedious business by the time you have got suitable loam, peat and other ingredients. Most shops selling garden products sell J.I. in large and small sacks and when you are using modest quantities it would seem best to purchase it ready mixed. It should be mentioned, however, that the standard from one producer to the next will vary considerably depending on the quality of loam that is used, so it is well to find the man who offers the best quality and stay with him.

Where larger quantities are needed, possibly for potting chrysanthemums, it may be better to mix your own, the following tables of requirements are offered. Loam comes from various sources, building sites among them, and it is advisable to get the best there is, not too heavy and not too thin, and to stack it for twelve months before it is used. There is much to be said for and against sterilization of the loam, but if it is stacked prior to use and kept weed-free it could well give better results than steamed soil.

The John Innes Seed Compost

Two parts loam
One part coarse sphagnum peat
One part coarse sand
1½oz (42g) superphosphate of lime
¾oz (21g) chalk (or ground limestone)
to each 28lb (12·5kg)

The seed mixture is suitable for seed sowing and for plants going into very small pots during the winter months, and may also be used for propagating new plants from cuttings.

John Innes Potting Compost No. 1

Seven parts loam
Three parts peat
Two parts coarse sand
¾oz (21g) chalk (or ground limestone)
4oz (112g) John Innes base fertilizer
per bushel (36l)

For young plants in 3 and 3½in (8, 9cm) pots, also for vigorous plants at first potting, and for plants being pricked out into seed boxes.

	Stove 65°F 18°C	Orchids, palms etc
	WARM CONDITIONS 55°F 13°C	Pot plants Early tomatoes Early seed sowing Root cuttings
	COOL CONDITIONS Frost free not less than 45°F 17°C	Over wintering many pot plants Dahlias Chrysanthemums Later sowings and plantings of all crops
	COLD CONDITIONS No heat	Almost hardy fruit Later start than above but earlier finish Over wintering doubtful

Plants for different heat levels

John Innes Potting Compost No. 2

The same ingredients as for J.I. No. 1 except for the base fertilizer which is increased to 8oz (224g), and the amount of chalk which is also doubled to 1½oz (42g).

For potting plants into intermediate size pots of 4½ and 5in (11, 12cm) diameter, and for more vigorous subjects such as cucumbers and marrows.

John Innes Potting Compost No. 3

Again the same ingredients except for chalk and fertilizer; the base fertilizer is increased to 12oz (336g) and the chalk to 2½oz (70g).

This mixture is used for all plants going into their final pots, that is to say pots between 7 and 10in (18, 25cm) in diameter. Also used for fruiting plants such as aubergines, capsicums, melons and tomatoes.

There are many substitutes on offer, but for the larger plant pots J.I. No. 3 is best, although additional peat may be required if the loam used is on the heavy side or if the plants being potted are known to have a finer root system.

Sterile sphagnum peat is the best as sedge is finer and makes a less open mix. The peat must be thoroughly soaked prior to being used, and if the peat comes in a large bale with a polythene wrap the best method of soaking it is to cut a hole in the top and bottom of the polythene, to put a hose-pipe in the top, and allow the water thoroughly to

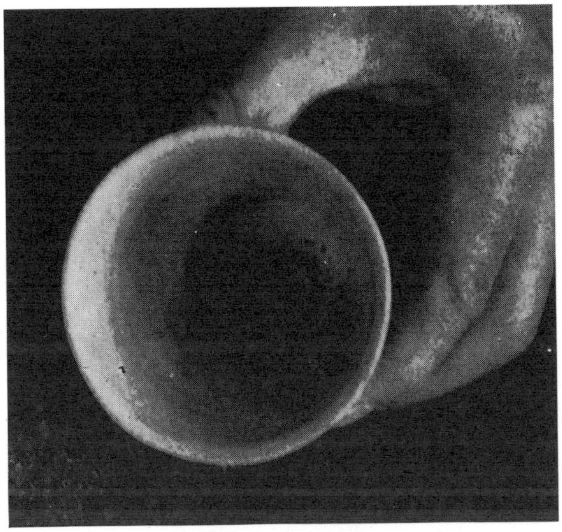

Potting up a chrysanthemum

Humex Tricklematic system (courtesy of Humex)

soak the peat. If the bale is broken open it is much more difficult to get the peat properly moistened.

There seems no need to give the constituents of the J.I. base fertilizer as it is available in almost all garden shops. There are also the soilless peat growing mixes, which have no loam in them, and are excellent for almost all plants in smaller pots. Many larger pots also, but my experience suggests that plants that are destined to be in pots for some time, as larger plants usually are, do better if potted into a mix with a little more body to it— the heavier medium will also offer top-heavy taller plants a little more stability.

Potting

When it comes to the actual potting operation the compost should be moist before use, and if a handful is compressed and the hand opened the mixture should not lie as a heavy, sodden lump in the hand. If the compost remains tightly compacted it will be wise, even at that late stage, to add a little extra peat in order to lighten the mixture unless the plants to be potted are known to prefer a heavy mixture. The reason for preferring a lighter compost for the majority of potted plants is that most of them must have a free draining mixture if the plants are to prosper, and heavy soil tends to be much slower to drain.

When potting, whatever the plant may be, it is wise to ensure that it is well-rooted in its present box or pot before attempting to move it on into something larger. And the new container must always be only a little larger than the pot which the plant is being transferred from, even though it may seem a waste of effort and involve a lot more potting operations than would seem necessary. Place a layer of 'crocks' (broken pieces of flower pot) in the bottom of the container to improve drainage, then enough compost to bring the pot ball to about the same height as it was in the previous pot then fill in the space around the sides with compost. There is no need to use roughage on top of the crocks as one did in the past, but it would be wise to break the hard crust of soil that has in all probability formed on the root ball of the plant that is being potted on. To get the plant out of its existing pot, hold the plant between two fingers at soil level, invert the pot, and give it a sharp tap against a firm object (for example the staging). If there are a mass of roots round the edge of the soil ball, it is time to pot-on. A stick may be needed to pack the soil gently in between the root ball and the sides of the new pot, but there should be no necessity for standing on your toes and ramming the soil into position with all your strength—the new roots will have trouble enough getting under way in the new compost without discouraging them by making the compost too hard, and impossible for roots to penetrate.

After potting the compost is well watered and left on the dry side for several days before watering again, and the pot is placed in a shaded part of the greenhouse until it re-establishes. At all costs avoid potting the plant into a container that is too large, never pot them before they are ready to be potted, but by the same token never allow plants to become starved through staying too long in the same pot. Definite rules cannot be laid down as to when plants should and should not be potted as some, like the sansevieria, can stay in the pot until they actually break it, whereas vigorous cinerarias and fuchsias can be potted several times over the spring and summer months. Also, when a batch of plants in small pots have just been potted they will do very much better if the pots are placed with their sides touching (pot thick) initially.

Watering

How to make plants grow by watering them, how to make them shrivel up by not watering them enough, or how to kill them off by destroying the roots through keeping the plants permanently sodden. You will see that there are many aspects of watering, some good and some very bad, and the problem is that it is extremely difficult to instruct anyone how they should go about the business of ensuring that their plants get the correct amount of moisture. Too wet and most will die, too dry and again most will die, so there must be that elusive happy medium somewhere along the line. Even the same sort of plants growing in different types of pot will require differing amounts of water—a plant in a clay pot growing alongside an identical plant in a plastic pot will probably need to be watered twice as often as its neighbour. The differing requirements of plastic and clay pots are worth noting if there is a general mixture of the different types of pots in your greenhouse.

A plastic water butt can be very useful

Seedlings, newly potted plants, and plants in small pots need to be watered with a can with a fine rose attached—in fact, when the can and fine rose is out it will be little extra effort to damp down the path and run a little moisture between all the pots in the greenhouse. By maintaining a humid, moist atmosphere when the greenhouse is warm by regular damping down, the feeling of the house will be greatly improved and the plant pots themselves will not have to be watered quite so frequently. When watering larger, established pots it is best to direct the spout of the can into the top of the pot and to fill the pot to its brim, repeating the dose if the plant is obviously in need of it. When watering the water should be seen to drain quite freely through the compost, and if it should fail to do so and lie on top of the soil then a check for the reason should be made. The most usual cause of blocked drainage is an accumulation of worm casts in the hole in the bottom of the pot which will prevent the surplus water draining away. The answer is to clean away the worm cast, find the worms in the soil and dispose of them, then wash the crocks before putting them back into the bottom of the pot. The plant can then be

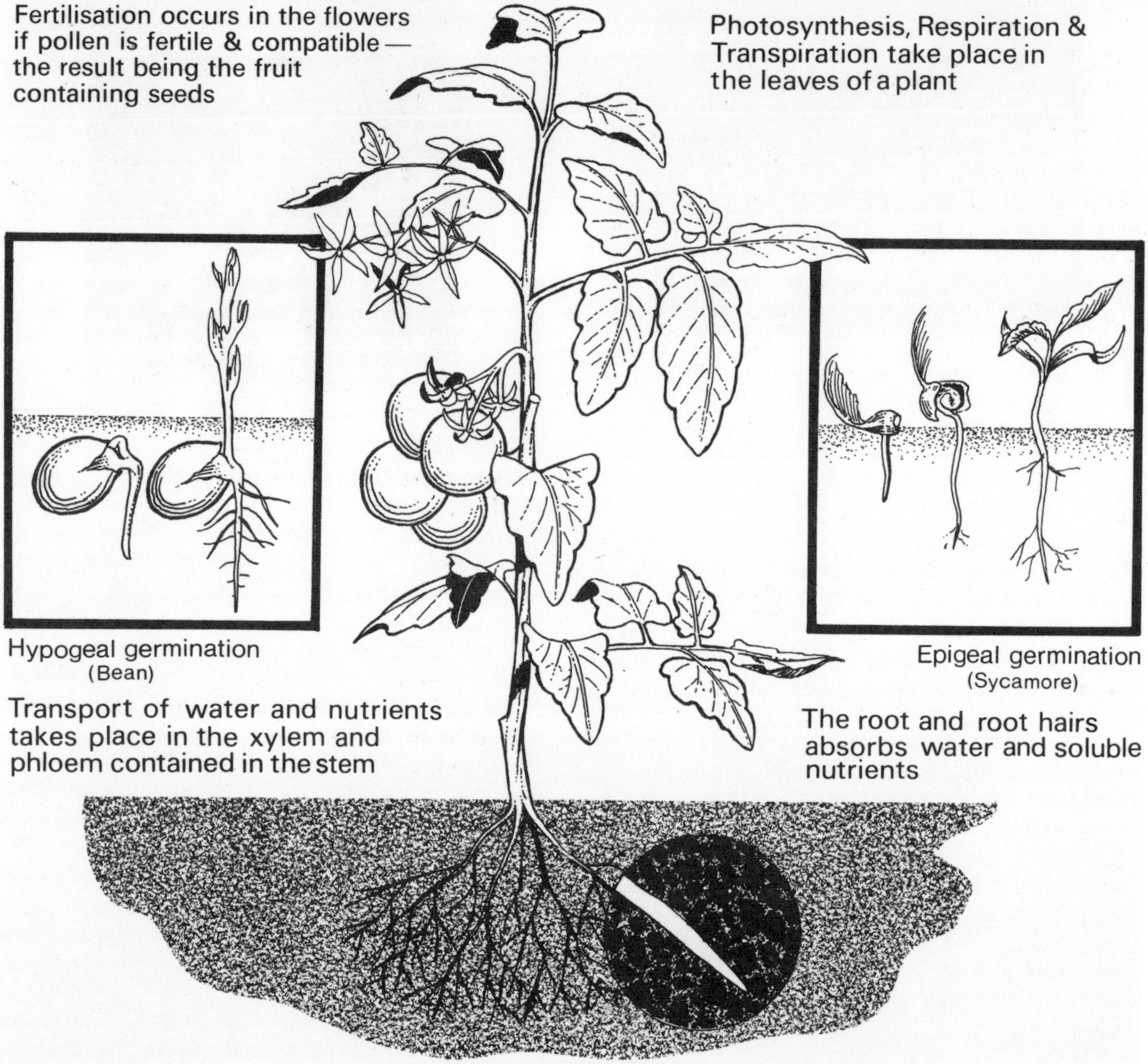

Diagram showing germination, transpiration and fertilization

Quisqualis indica makes a stunning greenhouse shrub

returned to its pot, but if it is excessively wet, then it will be advisable to stand the root ball on the upturned pot until such time as it dries out. It also helps to make a periodic duty of going around with a pointed stick and disturbing the crust of soil that usually forms on the soil surface of plants that have been in the same containers for some time.

For some subjects, if only to allay your personal misgivings, it may be as well to use rain water from the butt that has been catching surplus rain off the greenhouse roof to water plants such as azaleas and camellias. But it really is not essential as mine are years old and seldom see rain water!

Light, shade, and food

The need for good light and to shade plants from the sun if necessary has already been mentioned, but it will do no harm to repeat the message here. Providing plants with good light in which to grow is of extreme importance and is one good reason for locating the greenhouse well away from overhanging trees, or from the deep shadows cast by buildings. In poor light plants produce long, etiolated growth that is both unattractive and weak, making it almost impossible to grow plants of real quality. Plants will be similarly affected if shading is applied too heavily, or if shading is left on the greenhouse too far into the autumn. Shading blinds and rush matting shading have an advantage here in that these can be removed even on a dull day in order to provide plants with more light, but it is not so simple with more permament shading applied directly onto the glass. Under normal circumstance the first light flick of shading is put on towards the end of March, and as the suns rays intensify a further application is given. It will be messy, but when put on with a syringe a suitable dappled effect can be achieved, whereas when it is applied more simply with a distemper brush there is a blanket effect which, for many plants, cuts out too much light. Towards the end of September there should be very little shading left on the glass and any that may be present is best removed. Following removal of shading there may still be very hot, sunny days, and it is wise then to protect the odd more delicate plant with a sheet of newspaper supported above it. If you have a mixture of plants that need shade and full light, then it may be time to acquire another greenhouse so that they can both be given the particular conditions they require!

Feeding Feeding of established plants is something that is either totally neglected, or else the plants are fed so much that it is overdone to the detriment of the plant. Roots of plants should have filled their pots reasonably well, not have just a wispy few showing through the bottom or round the sides, before feeding begins. It is then wise to start with a weaker dilution or amount than the manufacturer recommends, and to increase it gradually until the full strength is being given. There seems little point in recommending particular fertilizers for particular plants, as there are so many excellent balanced plant feeding mixtures on the market with full directions telling one how the product should be used, and for which plants. And everyone swears by some particular brand or other—the really important thing to my mind is to abide by the directions on the bottle, packet, or whatever, and not to give plants excessive doses in the belief that you must be doing the plant more good. A maxim with feeding is that little and often is a much better practice than giving plants heavy applications occasionally. Plants in the greenhouse will need feeding, on the whole, during the spring and summer months if they are permanent members of the display. Also, plants that are dormant in winter will need no feeding and very little watering during this time—in fact, during the winter months when temperatures are lower in the greenhouse it is better to err on the dry side when watering the majority of plants.

In order to survive plants must have oxygen around their roots as well as in the atmosphere and when you water plants to the point of total saturation and never allow the mix to dry out in the slightest degree then all the air is excluded from the soil and an anaerobic or airless condition

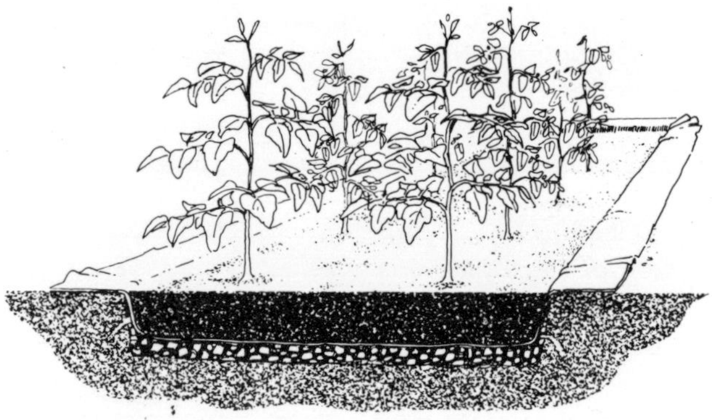

A simple hydroponics system

is set up. The result is that the roots begin to rot and die and the consequence of this is that the leaves in time react and turn brown, spotty, or something equally unattractive before they give up the ghost and drop off. So there is a lesson to be learned there in that plants should be watered and the mix allowed to dry a little before they are watered again. Avoid bone dry conditions, however, and be careful with such plants as azaleas and hydrangeas to ensure that they receive sufficient water.

Hydroponics

Having mentioned the possibility of failure if one gives plants too much water, we now come on to the subject of hydroponics—the science of growing plants entirely in water with a nutrient solution added to maintain plant growth. For many years experiments have gone on with this form of culture, but it has never at any time been the scene that the amateur enthusiast in his or her garden greenhouse could enjoy. The reason for this is that the water and solution in which plants were growing had to be frequently checked and analyzed to ensure that the nutrient was being held at the desired level—as we have seen all too often, too much or too little can be utterly disastrous.

Recently, however, the entire concept has come well within the range of the average householder with their windowsill plants, far more for the greenhouse owner who should, in theory, be doing a much better job of it. The change came when the Bayer Chemical Company perfected a new fertilizer specially for plants growing in water, known as Lewatit H.D.5 ion exchange fertilizer, with brown-sugar-like granules bonded on to polystyrene. So far the new feed appears to be quite foolproof in that one cannot overfeed or underfeed plants, as just the right amount of nutrient required by the plant is released into the water as it is needed. However, there is no release of fertilizer if rain water or very soft water is used. Tap water, or rain water with a little conventional fertilizer is required to ensure that there is a chemical present to act as a catalyst and provide the interaction that is needed.

To simplify things it may be as well to go through the process that is at present followed on a commercial nursery to convert plants from conventional soil growing to water culture. Although it is possible to grow from scratch by propagating cuttings in water before introducing them to water containing nutrients, the best results are achieved by first allowing plants to become established in soil before washing all the soil (it is important that there should be no trace of soil left around the roots) from the roots and potting the plant in a special pot in Hydroleca pebbles. Some explanation here—the special pot is one that has additional drainage holes in the base, and 3in (8cm) slits cut in the side of the pot from the base upwards, four slits cut with a hacksaw will be enough. The extra holes and slits will ensure that water is freely allowed into the pot. The plant must have some medium or other to keep it erect and this is where the Hydroleca (pebbles about the size of shelled hazelnuts and manufactured from London blue clay) comes in—the pebbles are porous, lightweight and attractive in colour. Plants quickly become stable as roots that are large, white and succulent grow around and amongst the pebbles.

The plant must never be potted too deeply—all leaf stalks and leaves must be above the surface of the Hydroleca. When potted the plant is ready to be placed in a 3in (8cm) depth of circulating water that is kept on the move by means of pumps and left for about two months to adjust properly to the new water roots which develop. The water has a special nutrient added on which the plants will feed during this initial period and requires regular checking to ensure that the balance is correct. Once established the plant is ready to be transferred to a decorative outer container to grow on in static water to which H.D.5 fertilizer has been added. Besides the fertilizer, plant and infilling of Hydroleca pebbles the container will also have a water-level indicator which is a simple guide for ascertaining that there is sufficient water in the container. The lower part of the plant pot should stand in about 3in (8cm) of water when the

A wick watering system

container is filled to the indicated ideal level. The indicating needle should be allowed to drop to the minimum mark before the container is replenished. This will ensure that air is getting to the lower part of the roots of the plant—and this is the secret of the success of the present improvement in hydroponics, that there is always ample air around the roots of the plant to keep it in good fettle.

The amount of fertilizer required depends on the surface area of the container, but small containers require fertilizer every six months, and larger ones on average every twelve months. What sort of plants can be grown by the new method, is a frequent question and the answer is, really, almost anything. Sansevierias, cacti, all sorts of things, and not only do they grow, some of them almost get out of control once they are established. Possibly the best subjects are the aeroids which produce large fleshy roots—monsteras, spathiphyllums and philodendrons in general are especially well suited to water culture. Treatment of the plants, either in the greenhouse or the home, is the same as for the same plant if it were growing in compost with the possible exception that they will not tolerate quite so much bright sunlight because they produce lusher growth.

Converting your own plants to growing in water should not be too difficult if you have a container that is watertight and the right depth, Hydroleca pebbles, H.D.5 fertilizer and a water level indicator—kits are available for doing the converting. A word of warning should be given here however to say that precious plants and expensive ones should not be used to experiment with—try something simple like a spider plant to begin with. It will be more expendable if things go wrong.

Mist propagation – *Top:* type of mist nozzle used *Bottom:* the nozzle in action

4 Propagation

There is always an air of mystique about propagation and, though not so prevalent these days, in the past 'The Propagator' on the commercial nursery was someone you looked upon with a touch of awe as he performed his magical deeds. And with many of the more delicate sides of propagation the respect was fully justified. However, even if you are a beginner, you will be surprised at what you can do with good material in the agreeable conditions that prevail in a warm greenhouse. Contrary to common belief there are few plants that actually WANT to die—for some reason or other the majority are killed off, mostly from too little or too much attention. The same with propagation—the cuttings or whatever do not want to die, and they will not, if they are given reasonable care. As suggested earlier it can be good sense to purchase young plants and to grow them on if only a few plants of any particular variety are wanted, and by doing so you will be able to delay the heating of the greenhouse for several weeks if it is only used for part of the year. But the real enthusiast will think this a poor suggestion as he or she will want to do it all from scratch, be it from seed or cuttings or by any other means.

Basic principles

There are a few basic principles which apply to propagation, especially in respect of plants that are being increased by vegetative means—cuttings, for example. And my experience suggests that the best propagators invariably accumulate the most rubbish—they are very much more selective about what is actually chosen as material to go into their precious propagating beds and the rubbish, instead of rotting and dying in the beds, is accumulated at their feet. The moral is that they only choose the best by pre-selection, and by choosing the best you get the best results. So, let that be a beginning to your propagating venture—select the best pieces of the plant that are available and they will do very much better. Taking the best growth from the plant will mar its appearance and you may feel you can better afford the spotted and discoloured pieces—but it depends on what you want, you can't have your cake and eat it as well!

Having got the right material, be it a geranium, African violet or rubber plant you should remove it cleanly from the plant and trim the end that will go into the compost with a sharp knife. The next step for your cutting will be to prepare or purchase a suitable medium in which to put it and make the thing produce roots of its own. The John Innes seed mix will be fine for most things, or you can use clean peat to which sharp sand has been added, or the peat on its own—moisten it before using, but do avoid making it soggy and miserable. Have it just wet enough so that when you compress a fistful you can just squeeze moisture from between your fingers—if there is no moisture it is too dry, and if moisture runs freely then it is obviously too wet.

Now we have the cutting and the rooting medium—the next step is to find something to put it in. Almost any pot or box will do provided it is not too large, scrupulously clean (well scrubbed in fact) and is provided with some means of drainage. There is no need for crocks, but the old 'uns will use them anyway (!), and the propagating medium should be pressed gently into position. A can with fine rose attached is then used to water the mix, but do not overdo it.

Warmth and Moisture The next step is to find a place to put the pot or box where it can be left pretty well without attention to callus (heal) over and develop its own root system. You can

Propagators

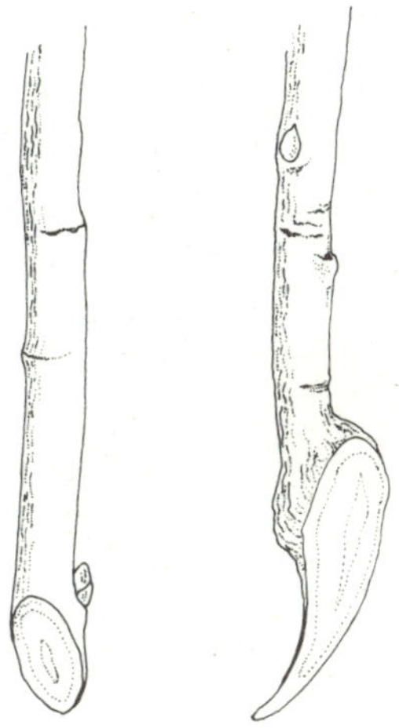

An internodal cutting and a hardwood cutting

take it that almost all the plants growing in the greenhouse will need warm and close conditions if cuttings of them are to root in reasonable time. It will also be beneficial if transpiration can be reduced to the minimum—as plants with roots transpire and give off moisture into the atmosphere the moisture is replaced from the soil through the root system. But as our poor little cutting gives off moisture into the atmosphere there are no roots so it is very quickly going to shrivel up and die if something is not done to get it out of trouble! And the way to do that is to put it in an airtight case which you can construct yourself without too much difficulty, or you can purchase a propagating case that has been specially made for the job. The odd few cuttings in pots can be placed in an airtight polythene bag, or if there are a lot of cuttings which root easily such as trandescantias or ivies, then they can be placed on the staging and a sheet of thin clear polythene placed directly on top of them. These cuttings will usually root with surprising speed and the only attention that is needed is a periodic lift of the polythene to ensure there is no rot setting up. However, once rooted it is important that the covering be removed permanently.

Another and more costly method of reducing transpiration is to instal a mist propagating unit which will provide a fine misting of water over the cuttings to reduce transpiration. The mist can be time set to come as and when you feel it is wanted, or an electronic leaf can be fitted which will activate the apparatus as the 'leaf' dries out. It will be a considerable aid to quicker rooting if the plants in their pots can be plunged in warm, moist peat, or if in boxes they can be placed on the peat.

Propagating ivy from tip cuttings

Taking a croton cutting

A further aid would be soil warming cables running through the peat—these are relatively cheap to run and well worth having in the small greenhouse. Even when potted, plants that have their pots plunged in peat heated by warming cables will grow very much better—plants seldom do well when they have 'cold feet'.

Maintaining an even temperature is also of the utmost importance, and one should aim for a minimum of 65°F (18°C) for the majority of greenhouses, more if the conditions are moist. With a propagating case and soil warming cables it should not be difficult to maintain the temperature suggested.

Given the foregoing conditions it should simply be a matter of keeping the cuttings clean by removing any dead leaves that may appear and keeping a watchful eye for mildew should the conditions become too wet. It is difficult to generalize, but most cuttings will take about six weeks to develop sufficient roots for them to be considered suitable for potting up, but there are those gardeners who feel that something must be happening the day after the cuttings are put in. They then go through the performance of digging them up at frequent intervals to see how they are getting on! With most aspects of gardening you have got to be patient and propagating cuttings is no exception—you have got to wait until the plant is good and ready to start growing. Avoid the temptation to pot them when they have made a few wispy roots, as it is much better to wait until the time when you can lift the cutting from the compost and there is a nice little clump of peat clinging around the base of it. And when they are ready be sure to put them into small pots of open mix to begin with.

Polythene wrap propagation

Easy subjects Among the easiest of cuttings to root are the tradescantias which could be a good subject for the beginner to tackle, and if grown well they make fine plants that will add colour and interest to any greenhouse. There are a number of colourful varieties and all can be increased from tip cuttings 3 to 4in (8 to 10cm) long, with up to seven cuttings being put in each $3\frac{1}{2}$in (9cm) pot. Other than being kept out of full sun, they have no special requirements. Impatiens, or Busy Lizzies, can be done in very much the same way, but one need not put so many cuttings in the pot. If a lot are required they can be put in rows in seed boxes and potted up when rooted. Similar treatment can be given to fuchsias of which almost any piece will root, and at almost any time of the year. Pelargoniums are also easy subjects, but it is advisable to prepare the cuttings and to leave them until the ends where they have been cut are completely dry before inserting in pots or boxes.

Leaf cuttings Cuttings from individual leaves are fascinating to do, and the most popular of all here is the saintpaulia, or African violet which is propagated by removing a complete leaf with its stalk. Any piece of stalk left may rot the plant so it is important to take it clean back to the crown of the plant. Firm, mature leaves are best and they should be cut cleanly with knife or razor blade before treating with rooting powder or liquid before inserting them in the peaty compost. You can root them in water only but the results are better if done in compost. Shallow boxes will suit them fine as containers, and it is important

Above: taking carnation cuttings

Left: planting a cutting. First a well-scrubbed pot is crocked to ensure rapid drainage. Some coarse peat is then placed over the crocks and this is then topped up with compost. The cutting is then prepared in this instance with a heel, shown at the tip of the knife. A hole is made in the compost with a dibble so that the heel will not get damaged as the cutting is pushed in and finally the cutting itself is inserted and the soil firmed

Taking geranium cuttings

that an absolute minimum temperature of not less than 65°F (18°C) is maintained. Keep them out of the sun, and when watering it is better to submerge the box in tepid water, and at all costs to keep water off the leaves themselves. When potting the cluster of plantlets that will have developed around the base of the petiole (leaf stalk) they should be gently teased apart and pricked off into boxes as individual plants. Many of the peperomias can be treated in similar fashion, in particular *P. caperata* and *P. hederafolia*. There is also a variegated form of *caperata* which is in short supply. This shortage is doubtless due to the fact that when propagating, in order to retain the variegation a piece of the stem of the plant is needed as the variegation is not present in plants raised simply from leaf cuttings.

To see tiny *Begonia rex* leaves sprouting from older leaves that were cut into squares is surely the most fascinating aspect of all the propagating ventures that may be attempted in the warm greenhouse. And it need not be so difficult as it might appear at first sight—you select firm leaves from mature plants and lay them on a sheet of clean glass, then proceed to cut them up with a razor blade into sections a little larger than a postage stamp. Lay the pieces, coloured side uppermost, on a bed of moist peat with a little sand added and spray over occasionally with tepid water from a very fine rose. If the cuttings are in a box the rooting medium should rise to about ½in (1cm) from the top so that a sheet of glass can be placed over the box yet not be in contact with the leaves themselves. If the conditions are moist there will be no need to use weights of any kind to hold the leaves down, but one should keep a watchful eye for any rotting that may appear. If any is seen the best action is to remove the leaves that are affected to prevent rot spreading to other leaves in the box. New plants can also be raised by removing an entire leaf from the plant and cutting the larger veins along the back with a sharp knife before placing the leaf on the rooting medium and holding it in position with one or two pebbles. But the first method described is much more fascinating, and among your acquaintances you will surely seem to have the magic touch. Allow the plantlets to develop a little cluster of new leaves before using a pencil to tease the plant out of the mix and potting it into a thumb pot, using the same peaty mix that was used for propagating —John Innes seed mixture.

There are many fine dieffenbachias that are grown for their attractive foliage, and the best of these in respect of suitability for the smaller greenhouse and on account of its more durable nature is *D. exotica*. The interesting thing about the propagation of these is that when plants have lost many of their lower leaves the bare stems can be

Root cuttings

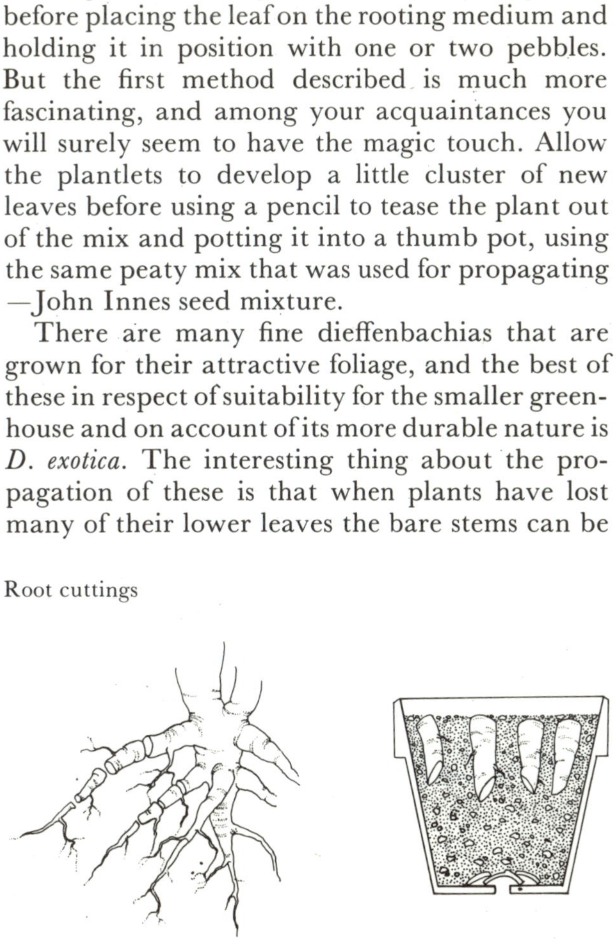

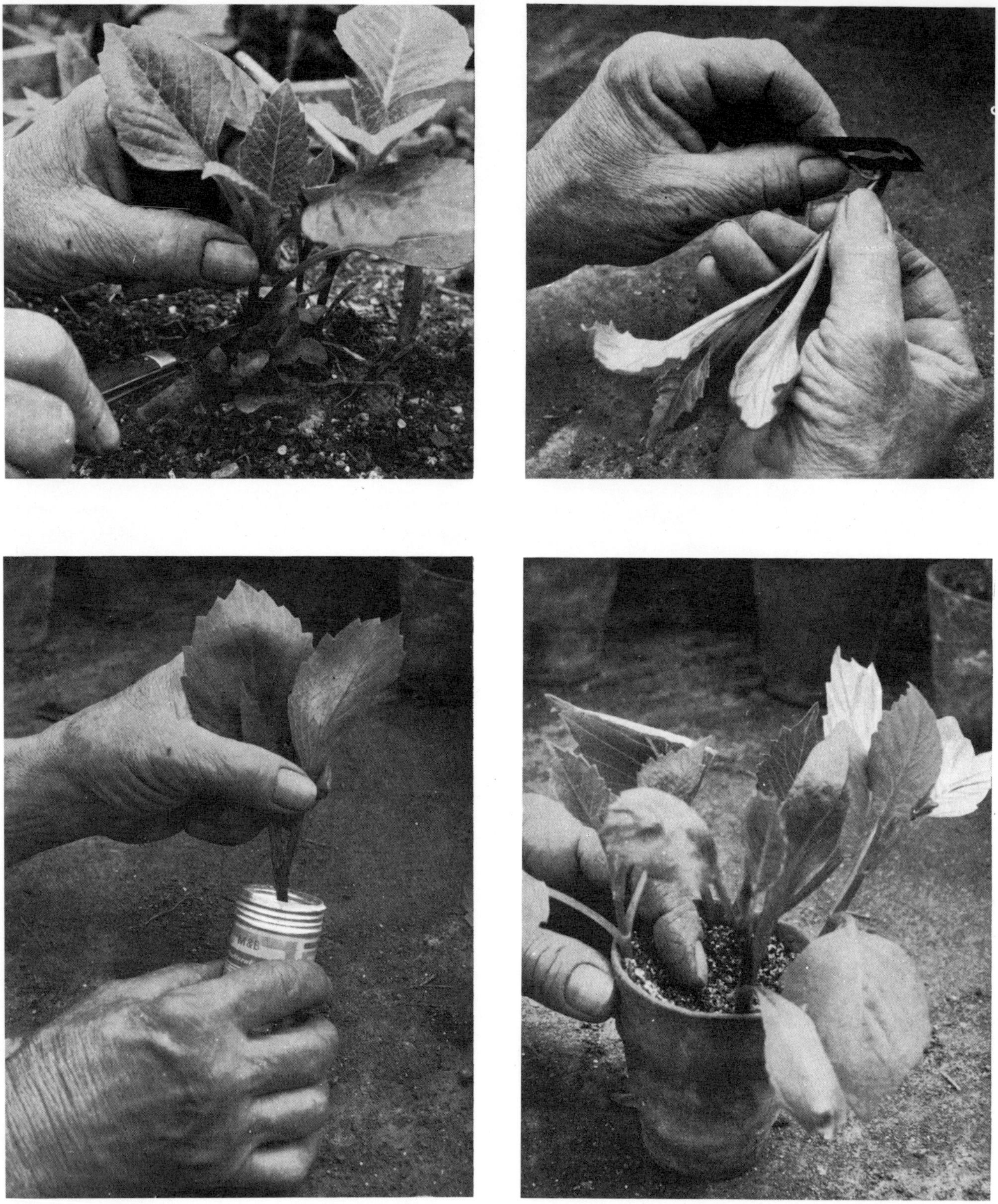

Taking dahlia cuttings

Increasing sansevieria by division

Air layering *Ficus elastica*. This is a technique of layering that is used basically on the principle that if you can't bring the branch to the earth you take the earth to the branch. First an upright slit is made in the branch. This is widened and then stuffed with sphagnum moss, wrapped with sphagnum moss and finally wrapped and sealed in an airtight polythene bag

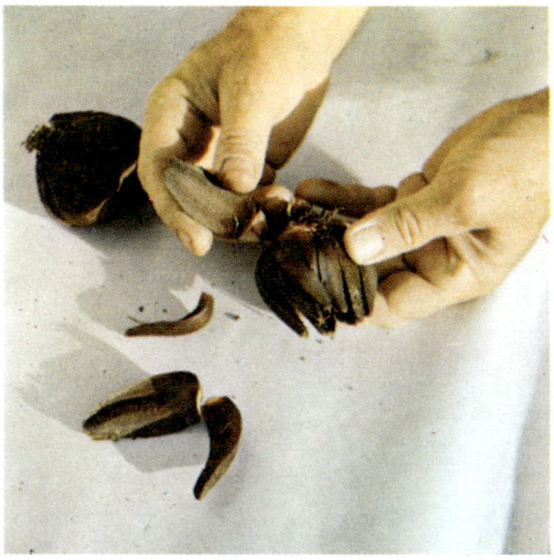

Lilies and related plants can be increased by removing the scales of which the bulb is composed and inserting the lower portion of each into a peaty compost. A new plant will then occur at the base of the scale

Lilies can also be increased by placing their auxiliary bulbs on a peaty compost

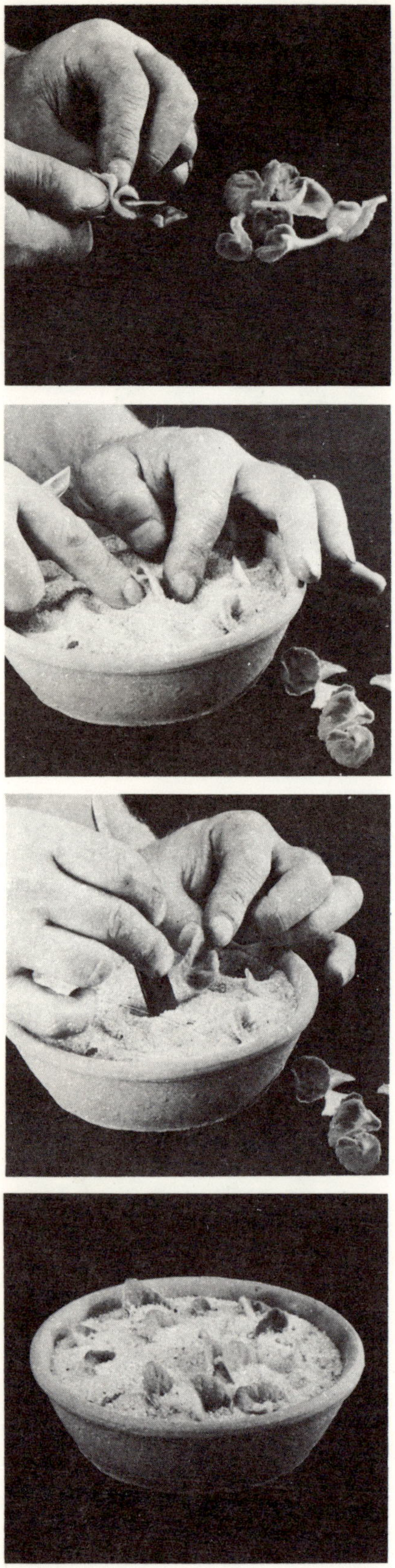

African violet leaf cuttings

cut into small sections about three inches long with a bud and partially buried in J.I. seed mixture—in a warm propagating case they will not be too much of a problem.

The temperature required by many of the more decorative foliaged dracaenas probably puts the possibility of growing them beyond the scope of the average small greenhouse owner. But that does not mean to say that you will not have any in the greenhouse, because you will have lots of friends who will have acquired dracaenas as houseplants, and as plants deteriorate indoors you will be asked to bring them back to their former glory in your greenhouse, however unsuited the house may be for this purpose. When the friend has left you can knock the plant out of its pot, and in all probability you will find that besides the finer roots there are thicker, much harder roots as well. The latter can be removed and cut up into sections about 1in (2·5cm) in length and treated in the same way as the dieffenbachia mentioned earlier. In this way the friend can have some of the new ones, and the propagator can also have some and no one will mind too much what happens to the older ailing plant.

For the outright beginner, possibly the easiest plant of all to increase is the chlorophytum, or spider plant, which produces perfect little plantlets on the ends of long stalks which sprout from the centre of the plant. Leave these until they are fairly well developed on the plant then remove them and put them direct into small pots with proper growing soil. Propagating the little plants is no problem, but some folk have difficulty in getting the parent plants to produce the little ones—the best advice here is to suggest that three medium size plants be put into a hanging basket to hang in the greenhouse and provide masses of cuttings. *Saxifraga sarmentosa* (Mother of thousands) is another attractive hanging plant which can be increased in very much the same way as the spider plant with very little bother.

Lilies can be easily increased by teasing away the scales from around the bulbs and planting them about half an inch deep in boxes of peaty compost in the autumn. Put them in a cold frame when established and by the following autumn the scales will have formed small bulbs at their base. Tuberous begonias can be increased by planting the corms in peat in February in the usual way, and cutting the corms into sections when one can see the growth buds. Care must be taken not to damage the buds, and each piece that is divided should have a growing bud. Dust the area that has

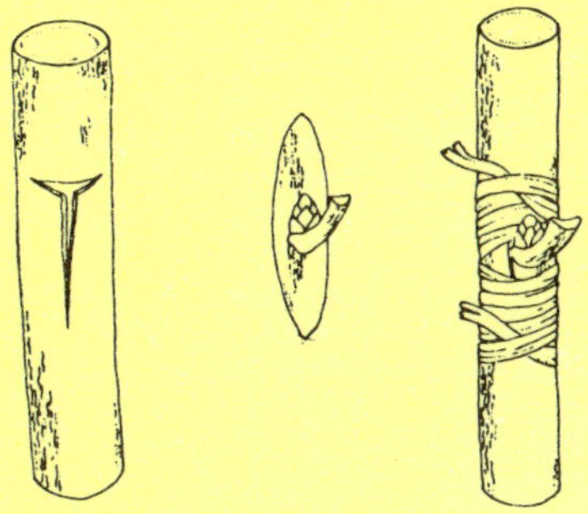

T-budding

Pricking out seedlings

been cut with charcoal before potting up or putting the pieces back into boxes to establish.

There are many fascinating bromeliads which can be propagated from seed that is fresh or from offsets that form around the base of the plant; *Aechmea rhodocyanea* is a good example. Freer growing plants that form larger clumps, such as *Billbergia nutans* can be increased simply by division—literally pulling the plant apart and potting up the resultant pieces individually.

The dear old aspidistra, cast iron plant, is another example of a plant that can be propagated by dividing established clumps into sections. Many of the ferns may also be treated in this way, as can *Spathiphyllum wallisii*, that lovely plant with glossy green leaves and creamy white spathe flowers.

Rubber plants can be propagated in the autumn by cutting the main stem of the plant up into sections, the prepared cutting to have one leaf and a piece of stem about 2in (5cm) long—care must be taken not to damage the leaf-bearing bud that will lie in the axil of leaf and stem. The top section of the plant may also be utilized for propagation, but the resulting plant is often less satisfactory.

In the greenhouse there will also be great opportunities for propagating all manner of plants from the garden—chrysanthemums, dahlias, geraniums, gazanias and many other plants that would otherwise have to be purchased annually.

Growing from seed

Other than acquiring plants by means of exchange, or simply winning them by accident as they drop into your hand on garden visits (!), the cheapest method of setting up a collection of plants is to grow them from seed. All sorts of exciting and interesting things can be done in this way—bird of paradise flowers that may take five years before they flower, so that you have little space for them and are probably fed up with the sight of the thing by the time the flowers appear. But when the flowers do emerge you will doubtless be the toast of the neighbourhood as all and sundry come to see the wonder of the age. You may be lucky enough to have your own banana plant from seed, and there should be few problems in raising exotic fruits such as lemons and oranges. With the latter the problem may in time be finding sufficient precious space in your greenhouse to accommodate them.

And this is the simple message all along the line when raising plants from seed in the greenhouse—the germination is almost invariably better than

Propagating unit with seedlings

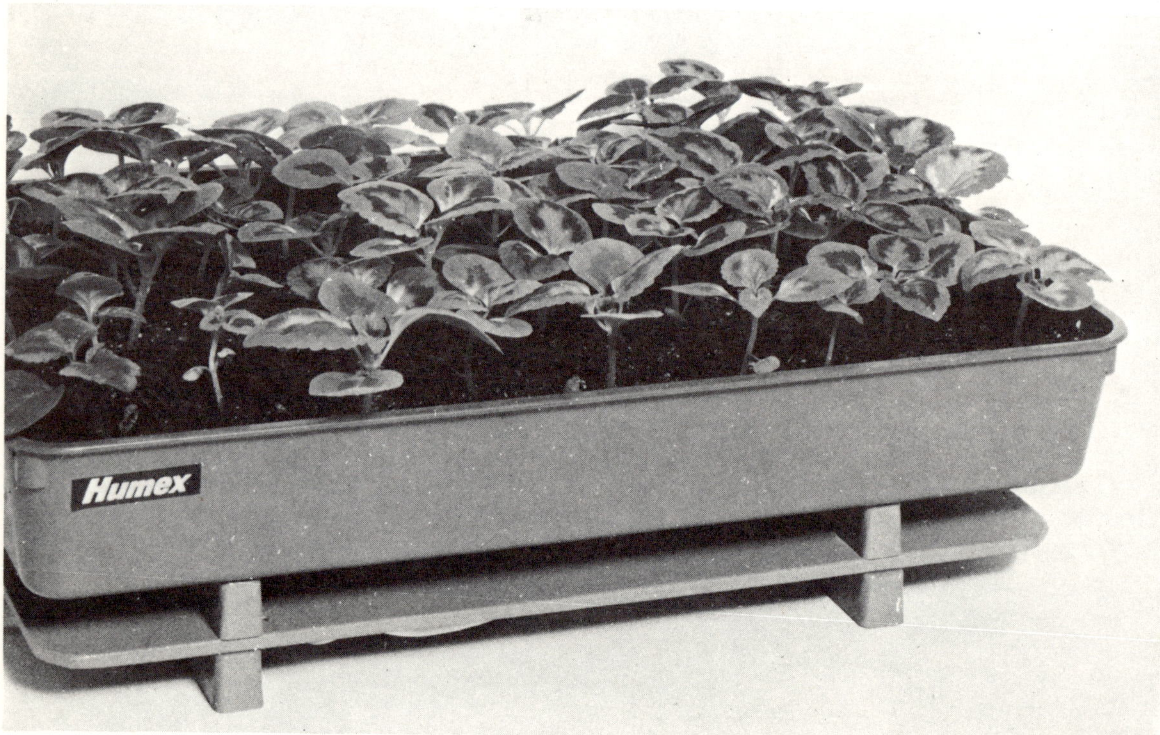

Morning Glory seedlings in Jiffy strips

one could possibly have hoped for, with the result that there is a surfeit of everything. You then have to forego all sentiment about caring for the poor things, you have got to be very firm and decide how many plants you can accommodate, and the rest have got to find another home, or they should go in the bin. Judging by my experience you will find it a bit hard to look at a box filled with beautiful young plants of cyclamen and make the decision that there is only space for twenty of them in the house and that the remainder must be got rid of. Sure, you can pot up and look after all these lovely plants, but the real question is, will you have room for them when they reach maturity and the greenhouse is overwintering all your other treasures as well? The simple answer is that you will not, and it is infinitely better to grow twenty super cyclamen plants than it is to have fifty scraggy things crowded into a space suitable for less than half that number so that none of them are any good. You will always have more seedlings than you need, so it is wise to weed out and dispose of the poorer ones as you go along. Every packet of seed you will ever buy will have explicit instructions concerning sowing and time of sowing on the packet so there seems little point in offering a lengthy list here of when things should be done.

Purchase seed from the source that you know to be reliable, and sow when and as directed. The important aspect as far as the greenhouse owner is concerned is to provide the right conditions and to do the ground work well. This will certainly mean hygenic conditions—washing down the inside of the greenhouse if there is a lot to be done (with bedding plants for example) and thoroughly scrubbing the seed boxes, and ensuring that the compost is right for the job. Most seed will germinate better if a sheet of glass is placed over the box after sowing and a sheet of newspaper over the glass until such time as the seeds germinate when it must be removed. At all costs avoid dank, stuffy conditions in the house by airing on every occasion that the weather permits—in dank conditions seedlings are more liable to be affected by damping off which rots the base of the stem. A final word—when the seed has been sown put a label in the box indicating the variety, date of sowing and from whom the seed was purchased. Besides the labelling it is not such a bad idea to have a hard-covered notebook for recording all the operations in the greenhouse—you will then have a complete record of the suppliers of the seed that provided the best plants, and a host of other interesting information into the bargain.

5 Foliage and Flowering Plants

The growing of foliage and flowering plants in the small hobby greenhouse is pure luxury, something that is done for the sheer pleasure of having beautiful things around you. Besides the cost it will take endless time but, for the lover of plants, there is little that compares with standing in a colourful, well-filled greenhouse knowing that you are responsible for what exists around you. The maintenance of such a greenhouse is seldom a task for the beginner, as the skills required are the sort that are acquired with experience over the years.

In the following pages most of the more common pot plants are mentioned, and many of the less usual, with more emphasis being given to the plants that are generally considered to be important. All of them are dealt with in their respective families so saving endless repetition, as many of

Strong but lightweight cedarwood staging gives ideal support for plants

the plants within the various families require similar cultural treatment. If you know you want to find a particular plant and do not know its family name, it will be listed by its ordinary name in the index.

Acanthaceae

There are a number of fine aphelandras in this family, but the only two that are likely to be available are *A. squarrosa Louisae* and *A.* '*dania*'. Both have colourful yellow bracts, with those of the former being more showy, and green leaves that are attractively marked in silver. *A. dania* is shorter and more compact, but it is inevitable that in time plants will become leggy and unattractive—it is then best to cut the main stem back to a stout pair of leaves which will encourage the development of side growths that can be used for propagating fresh plants. Once cuttings have been taken and are rooted the old plant should be disposed of.

Cuttings are best taken from growth that has developed two pairs of firm young leaves inserted in peaty compost. Once rooted they must be potted into John Innes No. 3, and when roots show through to the sides of the pot feeding must begin. Any neglect of feeding will quickly result in leaf discolouration. Keep in good light but avoid strong, direct sunlight, and maintain a temperature in the region of 60°F (15°C).

Nerium oleander makes an attractive pot plant

Beloperone guttata Native to Mexico, this plant has only come into its own in the past 25 years, and is best known by its common name of shrimp plant—the bracts are brownish orange in colour and in appearance they resemble shrimps. Light, temperature, growing mix and feeding requirements are the same as suggested for the aphelandra. Plants should be potted on as soon as

Peat pots with seedlings

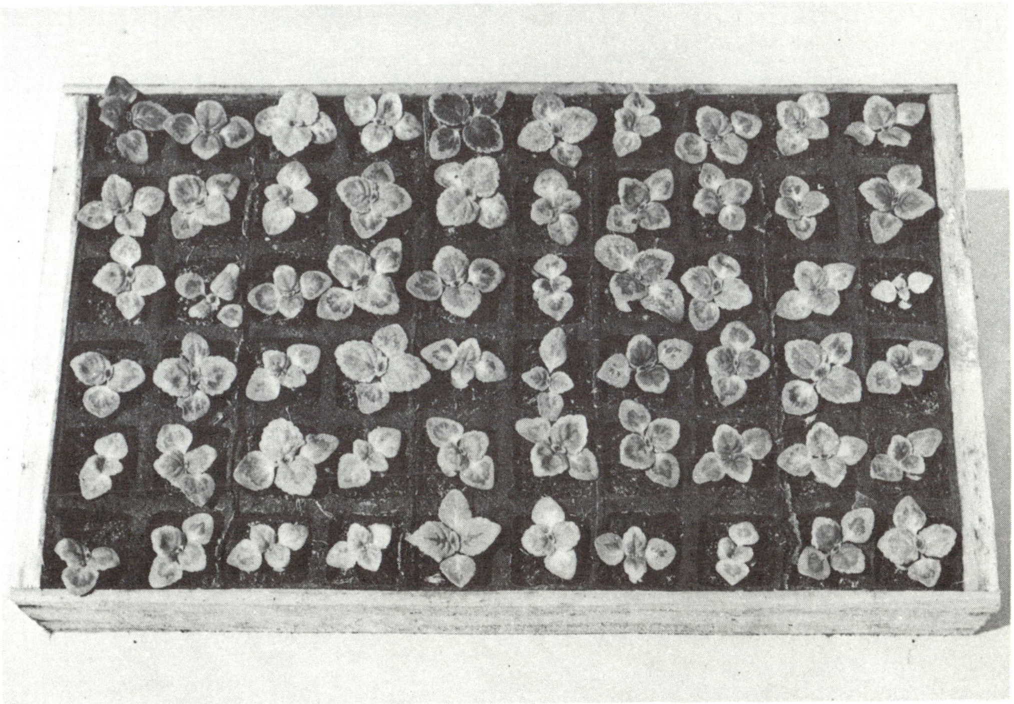

Allamanda cathartica is an impressive member of the Apocynaceae family

they have filled their existing pots with roots, provided it is not in the middle of winter which is never the best time for potting operations.

Young plants will tend to produce their attractive bracts in profusion, often to the detriment of the plant which is weakened through producing too many. If larger plants are wanted it is much better to remove the earlier bracts so that the plant may become more prolific in leaf production, so enabling it to bear a greater than usual number of bracts when it is older. Untidy plants may be trimmed to shape at almost any time, and trimmings a few inches in lengh may be used as cuttings, putting several pieces to each pot of peaty compost.

Apocynaceae

Mature plants with roots confined to 10in (25cm) pots reach a height of some 8ft (2·4m), so they are only suited to the larger greenhouse. Scented flowers in single and double forms are borne on tall stems of narrow, evergreen leaves and flower at intervals during the summer months. Remove any shoots that form at the base of flower trusses otherwise the flowers will be starved of nourishment. Ample watering and regular spraying of foliage is necessary during the summer months, as is regular feeding. Keep on the dry side in winter when the temperature should not fall below 45°F (7°C). Plants will tolerate full sunlight, but light shading will ease the watering problem. Firm cuttings about 5in (13cm) in length can be rooted in the spring at temperatures of around 65°F (18°C). In October after flowering, prune back the previous year's growth to about 6in (15cm) from the base.

Asclepiadaceae

Ceropegia woodii is a fascinating trailing plant for the small greenhouse, having slender stems carrying enchanting heart-shaped leaves that are fleshy in texture. When temperatures are on the low side give less water, otherwise a very accommodating plant that will tolerate a variety of conditions. Grow in light shade and keep in smallish pots, and propagate from single leaves with a piece of the slender stem attached. Plants will trail for several feet, but can be trimmed back at any time.

Where a temperature of not less than 55°F (13°C) can be maintained in winter, *Stephanotis floribunda* is one of the most prolific climbing greenhouse plants. There is an inevitable leaf drop in winter when soil is kept on the dry side, but this should not give rise for concern as there is abundant growth in the spring. To restrict growth roots should be confined to large pots, and this in turn may result in a more plentiful supply of flowers which are often sparse when leaf growth is too vigorous. Tubular flowers are borne in clusters and have an almost overpowering scent. Lime-free growing mix is essential and invasive growth can be cut back to shape in early spring, when the plant can be thoroughly cleaned out and trained

You can increase many foliage and flowering plants by taking cuttings; a good and a bad example are given here

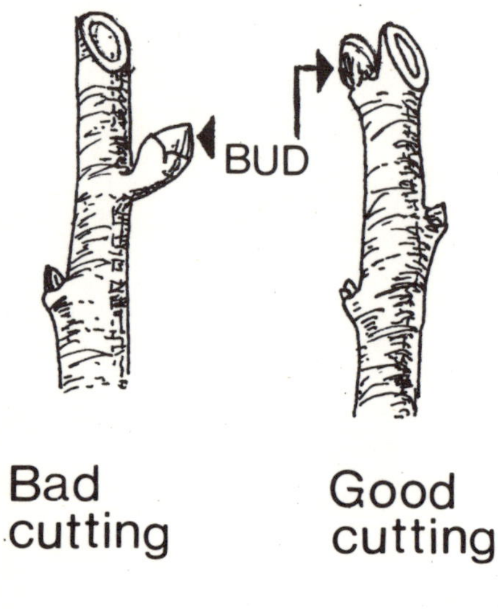

up to the top of the house. Mealy bug and scale can be troublesome pests, but both can be eradicated by thorough spraying at regular intervals with malathion.

Hoya carnosa has pendulous clusters of the most fascinating wax-like flowers that are, alas, seldom very plentiful. Conditions are similar to those needed for the stephanotis, but on account of its rapid growth it would be unwise to have both in the same house. Keep well-fed and well-watered in spring and summer and on the dry side in winter, and feed when plants are actively growing.

Both plants may be increased from spring cuttings taken from older growth. The stephanotis will occasionally develop large and interesting seed pods which should be left on the plant until fully ripe when the pod will split open and expose the most stunning white, silken parachutes to which the seeds are attached. In reasonable warmth seed will germinate freely, although plants take a long time to reach flowering size.

Araceae

The large aeroid family provides many of our finest foliage plants, also a number of exciting flowering subjects, all of which require temperatures of not less than 60°F (15°C) and conditions that are as humid as possible. All require moist root conditions and fairly heavy shade, also a peaty, open mix when potting. Restricting root development by confining them to pots will reduce the amount of top growth of the more vigorous philodendrons which, given a free run,

Amorphophallus titanum is an unusual and impressive plant for the large greenhouse

Philodendron erubescens

would be quite capable of filling the small greenhouse with foliage.

Many produce aerial roots along their stems and as they lengthen these should be neatly tied to the main stem of the plant to prevent them untidily rambling over the staging. Many of the aeroids, monsteras for example, can be grown from seed sown in warm conditions or from cuttings in a closed propagating case. Occasional cleaning of leaves of plants with natural glossy leaves will improve their appearance, but this treatment need not be given too often—every six months or so. Most of the plants in this family seem to be especially well suited to the practice of growing plants in water with a nutrient solution added—in particular spathiphyllums do amazingly well.

Anthurium andreanum (Painter's palette) and *A. scherzerianum* are both exotic flowering plants, the latter being more compact and better suited to the small greenhouse, while the former produces stately blooms on stems 2ft (60cm) or more in length. As *A. andreanum* increases in height it is wise to bind a good thickness of wet sphagnum moss that has been soaked in liquid fertilizer around the stem of the plant—if the moss is kept moist the plant will develop much healthier growth. The smaller plant attains a height of about 18in (45cm) and the taller one in the region of 3 to 4ft (90 to 120cm). Grown purely for its foliage, *A. crystallinum* has superbly patterned heart-shaped leaves and requires a growing mix that is very free draining. Mixing fresh sphagnum moss with the peaty medium will encourage freer root development.

The dumb canes, dieffenbachias, are all stately plants with beautifully marked foliage, and get their unusual common name from the fact that the sap getting onto a person's tongue will render them speechless as the tongue swells up. This is a highly unlikely occurrence, however, as the sap has a most unpleasant odour that will discourage most would-be tasters! Nonetheless, after cutting through the stems to take cuttings, for example, it is a wise precaution to wash afterwards. Most of these produce very insignificant spathe flowers that are best removed as they begin to open.

Of the larger green-foliaged plants the Swiss cheese plant, *Monstera deliciosa*, is the frontrunner in popularity and is without doubt the plant about which most questions are asked. Most of the plants produced on a commercial basis are grown from seed and, given the warmth and moisture they require, will attain majestic proportions in time and may even favour the owner by producing sweet-tasting monstera fruits. When stems need supporting a moss-covered stake should be placed in the centre of the pot to tie the plant and its aerial roots to—this will improve the appearance and the performance of the plant.

There are many splendid philodendrons to choose from, but it is wise to check the eventual height of the plant when it is acquired, otherwise the resulting growth could be an embarrassment. There are many with smaller leaves, and *P. scandens* with its small green, heart-shaped leaves is best known and a useful foil plant in the mixed house, or makes a good hanging basket plant. For the ambitious grower there is also *P. melanochryson*, which has small leaves with a brownish velvet appearance—this will trail or climb.

Two plants with creamy white spathe flowers are *Spathiphyllum wallisii* and *S.* × '*Mauna loa*', the former being a compact plant reaching a height of 18in (45cm) and the latter a plant with leaves 3ft (90cm) long and flower stems up to 4ft (120cm). The latter would be the maximum size and not the sort of development that one would expect in the small greenhouse unless the plant was growing on one of the hydroponic systems. The flowers last well when cut for decoration, and both sorts may be increased by dividing the clumps and potting up the resultant pieces individually in peaty compost.

Araliaceae

The principal plants here are the ivies—humble plants that offer numerous possibilities in that they are perfectly hardy, very useful for hanging baskets, planted bowls and for draping along

Begonia 'Firebrand' gives an impressive display

Begonia 'Mrs T. White'

the front of staging at official events. They do very much better in cooler conditions, as there is the distinct possibility of plants becoming infested with red spider if the greenhouse is too hot and stuffy. There is also a fascinating selection of plants with both green and variegated leaves, and when they have outlived their stay in the greenhouse they can be planted in the garden for cuttings to be taken as required. Out of doors there can be few better plants than *Hedera canariensis* with its large green and cream leaves that are ideal as ground cover, for covering unsightly objects, or simply climbing a wall. All the ivies will root readily from cuttings taken at any time and put several to each pot.

Aralia sieboldii (Fatsia japonica) has large green leaves and is a fine plant where space is ample—it is also hardy out of doors. The cross between the aralia and hedera is aptly named *Fatshedera*, but is a little more difficult to maintain in good order, although a fine subject when something tall and stately is required. The aralia is raised from seed and the fatshedera from pieces of stem with a single leaf attached.

As a complete contrast, *Aralia elegantissima*, with its upright growth and delicate, almost black leaves will test the skill of the most accomplished greenhouse owner. Shaded conditions and temperature of not less than 65°F (18°C) are essential if you are to hope to be successful. Plants attain tree proportions in time, but in average conditions will shed their leaves and give up the ghost long before you need fear the glass being pushed off the house!

Begoniaceae

For a spectacular display there are few plants that compare with the tuberous begonias: the pendulous ones for hanging baskets and the upright ones for 7in (18cm) pots. These may be raised from very fine seed sown at the beginning of the year in high temperatures around 75°F (34°C)—great care is needed when handling and potting seedlings. Where high temperatures cannot be maintained tubers may be purchased and planted in boxes of peat and sand in late February, the rounded part of the corm being pressed into the compost which must be well moistened. When a reasonable amount of growth has been made the tubers should be potted into 5in (13cm) pots using J.I. No. 2 mix—to encourage maximum rooting the tuber should be buried. Strong-growing plants can later be potted into 7in (13cm) pots using the same grade mix. Heavy growth will mean the need for adequate staking, and when flowers appear the smaller female flowers which appear alongside the larger male ones should be removed in order to encourage larger flowers. In dank airless conditions the botrytis fungus can be troublesome to the majority of begonias in the greenhouse. Growing mix must be kept moist, but avoid saturation and ensure that the pots are adequately drained. In autumn as the foliage begins to yellow and deteriorate water should be gradually withheld until the mix is dry, when the tubers can be shaken free of soil before storing in dry peat in a warm place for the winter. Tubers of pendulous varieties are treated in exactly the

Begonias come in a very wide range of colours

same way, except that they are planted in hanging baskets rather than pots, although pots with single plants can be suspended from the ceiling if there is insufficient space for baskets.

The rex begonias are grown purely for their beautiful leaves which are wonderfully marked and cover a wide colour range. Raised from leaf cuttings these require temperatures in the region of 60°F (14°C) and a moist, shaded greenhouse with a buoyant atmosphere. Useful for many purposes, they do especially well when placed just under the staging along the path and out of the way of oversize feet. Fungus diseases are again a problem, so a careful watch must be maintained for telltale spots on the leaves. *Begonia masoniana* has a distinctive German iron cross pattern in the centre of its leaves and provides a large and impressive plant when well cared for—treatment and conditions are the same as those for the rex begonia.

Then there are the cane type begonias, most of which are easy to propagate and care for, but demanding on space. Many of them, such as *B.* 'President Carnot', have the added benefit of pendulous clusters of colourful flowers for many months of the year.

Bromeliaceae

The pineapple is the best known of this family which offers a fantastic range of leaf colours, leaf shapes and flowering bracts that are so exotic they seem unreal. All of them originate from tropical South America and are mostly epiphytes, although there are some terrestials that grow amongst rocks. Some grow into small star-shaped plants, such as the cryptanthus, while others form massive rosettes of leaves with flesh-cutting spines along their outer margins. In spite of their many drawbacks the bromeliads are among the most fascinating of plants for the warmer greenhouse, and are not too demanding in respect of general care. Use an open peaty mix with pine needles added if these are available when potting, and never use

pots that are too large. As an alternative to pots many of the smaller plants, such as tillandsias, can have their roots wrapped in sphagnum moss before attaching them to pieces of tree bark and suspending them on thin wires from the greenhouse roof—an occasional soaking in a bucket of tepid water will keep them going.

Aechmea rhodocyiana (*A. fasciata*) is a popular variety with grey rosettes of leaves which form a natural watertight funnel, and an exotic pink bract with intense blue flowers. Once having flowered, the rosette-forming plants begin to deteriorate and eventually die when the flower has lost its attraction, but as this happens new young growth will appear at the base of the parent rosette. The old rosette can be cut away when it has lost its attractive appearance, but the young plants should be protected as they will flower in subsequent years. Alternatively, when the young plants have attained reasonable size they can be cut from the parent and potted individually. Plants can be grown in light or shade and do not mind provided the temperature is maintained over 60°F (15°C).

Campanulaceae

When well grown, plants of the white campanula, (Star of Bethlehem) can be particularly attractive. There are also *Campanula isophylla* which is blue and *C. isophylla Mayi* which is mauve, but *C. isophylla alba*, the white form, is much the better, and easier to manage into the bargain. New plants can be raised from cuttings taken in the spring and

This and facing page: propagation of begonias by leaf cuttings

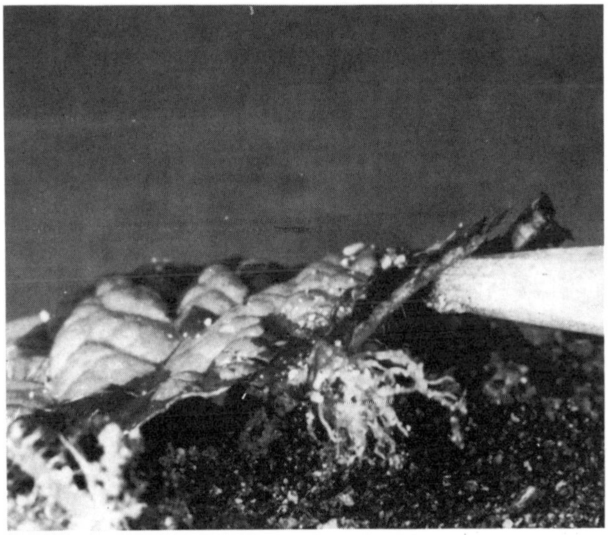

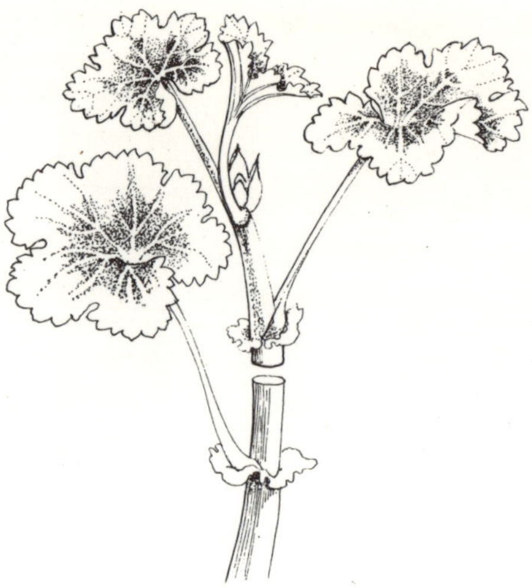

A softwood cutting

kept in a propagating case at around 60°F (15°C). Pot on into J.I. No. 1 mix and suspend plants from the roof of the house once they have become established. Provide light shading and water copiously once the plants have got under way, and remove any dead flowers regularly. In the autumn cut the foliage hard back to the top of the pot and store it in a warm and dry place until the spring when watering should start at the first sight of new growth. Once the mix is well moistened and plants are producing new leaves much of the old mix can be teased away from the roots, and the plants should be potted in fresh J.I. No. 1, in the same pot if need be.

Commelianaceae

Because of their cheapness and ease of propagation, the tradescantias are much despised in some circles. However, they are very rewarding, not to say useful, if given reasonable care. There are many different ones to choose from, but the majority will do well in the lightly shaded house if they are potted into J.I. No. 2 mix and kept watered and fed during the summer months of the year. It is frequently said that the variegation of the plant will improve if it is made to suffer by giving very little water and equally little feeding, but this is rubbish. The best way to grow them is to keep them on the move by first potting into reasonable pots or baskets and feeding once they are established and, to keep the variegation, the green shoots that appear should be removed immediately before they take over the entire plant. When they loose their attraction, older plants should be disposed of after the necessary cuttings have been taken and are rooted. As with the ivies, better plants will result if several cuttings are placed in each small pot.

Tradescantia 'quicksilver' has large silver and green leaves carried on stout stems, which make this one of the most striking members of the family. One of the most colourful of foliage plants when you take the time to study it is *Zebrina pendula*, which has a purple reverse and an upper surface that is a glistening silver and green. There are also plants with golden yellow and soft pink colours predominating.

Compositae

Once you give a plant a name and it sticks it is not easy to get rid of it again, and this seems to be the case with the cineraria, which should be more properly referred to as *Senecio cruentos*. The family are perennials, but are best treated as annuals, seed being sown in April, May and June—a little each month in order to give a longer period of blooming. Cool, lightly shaded conditions are ideal, and young plants once established can spend the summer months in a cold frame. Use J.I. No. 1 when potting and ensure that it is well drained—place the pots in the cold frame on slats of wood or upturned pots to prevent worms getting into the pot drainage holes. In the course of one season plants can be potted on as far as 10in (25cm) pots, with huge plants to show for your efforts, but it is probably better with the small greenhouse to purchase the *C. multiflora nana* strains to give showy plants in a much smaller area.

Pisonia brunoniana makes a striking greenhouse shrub

Cyperaceae

Few smaller greenhouses have the necessary space for accommodating pool features, but for those that have, papyrus plants would be an essential part of the setting—the two most likely plants would be *Cyperus diffusus* and *C. alternifolius* which attain a height of some 3ft and 7ft (90cm and 2m) respectively. Even without a formal pool setting both these plants with their umbrella topped flower stems have a great attraction and will do well in the average warm greenhouse if the pot in which the plant is growing stands permanently in a few inches of water. Such treatment would be certain death to almost all greenhouse pot plants, but the papyruses are natural water plants and revel in such treatment. Shaded, warm conditions suit them best and when increasing plants it is a simple matter of removing them from their pot and using a strong knife to cut away tufts of leaves with a part of the root system attached.

Ericaceae

The florist's azalea, *Rhododendron simsii*, is another plant that has resolutely stuck to its more popular name of *Azalea indicum*. Plants may be raised from firm cuttings inserted in peat and sand in a warm propagating case and kept moist by spraying from above. Getting plants of flowering size is a long process by this method and it is much better to purchase young grafted plants and to grow them on. Using a mixture of peat and leafmould plants can be potted on and may be kept for many years by having them in a frost-free greenhouse during the winter, then indoors while they are in flower, and plunged in a bed of peat in the garden in a shady place during the summer months. During the spring and summer, plants will require regular feeding with a balanced liquid fertilizer. The most important requirements are to prevent frost damage and to keep the growing mix wet at all times. If it is available, rain or soft water should be used, but in any event tap water will do no actual harm to your plants. When in flower, plants will retain their attractive colouring for a much longer period if the general conditions are cool rather than hot.

Geraniaceae

Accepting an invitation to judge the county flower show in my home town in the north of Scotland some years ago it took my breath away on entering the tent to see the remarkable standard that had been set. In the end a pelargonium of outstanding merit was given the premier award, and three similar plants were awarded the 'best in a class for three plants'. All four plants were from the same exhibitor—a farmer's wife whom under the circumstances, I would have expected to be a dedicated enthusiast for that particular type of plant. On enquiring however it transpired that the lady in question had only grown four plants for the show! Not only that—this judge was further shattered to hear from the astonishingly confident winner that she had just potted up the four plants she intended entering for the show the following year. Beat that for being sure of your capabilities.

Not difficult to manage, regal pelargoniums must have full light, and are kept on the dry side in winter and watered freely during spring and summer, when they should also be fed with a balanced liquid fertilizer. Cuttings of non-flowering young growth should be taken in early August, these to be about 4in (10cm) in length with the lower leaves removed and the severed ends treated with rooting powder before inserting. During August and early September plants can be placed in a sheltered position out of doors. Prior to placing outside the plants can be pruned to shape, all long and untidy growth being cut well back. Bring them into the greenhouse before the nights become too chilly, and in it maintain a minimum temperature of about 45°F (7°C). Zonal pelargoniums have dark rings in the centre of their green leaves and are mostly overwintered in the greenhouse so that they can be used in hanging baskets, window boxes, patio planters and summer bedding schemes when all possibility of frost has gone. These plants have undergone many changes in recent years and there are now many fine new American varieties available. With F_1 hybrid seed one also has the opportunity of sowing seed in the early spring to see them bloom during the summer months. Cuttings will root readily at almost any time, but many commercial nurserymen now root their cuttings early in the spring to have plants ready for sale in late May. There is a snag, however, in that cuttings are flown in from countries such as Portugal where stock is raised by specialist growers.

If you are short of propagating space, cuttings of zonal pelargoniums can be taken in late August, and the severed ends allowed to dry before inserting the cuttings in the open ground to be lifted and potted once they have rooted. To conserve green-

Pelargonium cuttings are not difficult to propagate

Codiaeum 'Emperor William'

house bench space plants can be severely cut back when they are taken back into the greenhouse in late August and in the spring the old soil can be removed from around the roots and the plant then potted up into fresh J.I. No. 2 mix. Surprisingly enough, plants can be packed on to the staging quite close together and come to little harm providing they are not overwatered.

The attractive ivy-leaved pelargoniums are equally easy to manage, but are at their best when seen in hanging baskets on their own, as there will then be no need to feed them and they will be a better colour as a result.

Euphorbiaceae

Without doubt the most colourful of all foliage plants is the codiaeum, or croton, with its multi-coloured leaves in many shades of orange, red and yellow. The flowers are insignificant and should be removed as they appear, unless you are interested in the possibility of saving seed from the plant. Adequate heating is an absolute must when growing codiaeums, as they will quickly shed their colourful leaves if the temperature remains below 60°F (15°C) for any length of time—temperatures between 60° and 70°F (15° and 21°C) would be ideal.

The best plants are raised from tip cuttings taken at any time of the year and placed in a propagator where the temperature does not fall much below 70°F (21°C). One or two lower leaves should be removed before inserting cuttings in small pots filled with J.I. No. 2 mix. The length of the cutting is immaterial as quite long pieces will root—with longer cuttings a better root development will be had if a few notches are made in the part of the cutting that is to be below soil level. Codiaeums are voracious feeders and will need J.I. No. 3 mix at the first potting, and frequent feeding thereafter—they quickly fill their pots with roots, so the feeding should not be too long delayed after potting. Full sun is also an essential requirement if plants are to retain their colourful foliage; in poor light leaves take on much greener, less colourful look. Plenty of water is also needed: more in summer than in winter, but the growing mix should at no time dry out.

In large pots codiaeums will become 10ft (3m) tall and 5ft (1·5m) across, but only in ideal conditions and you can always prune them back to a more managable size at any time of the year. Plants are usually available in small pots, but it may be necessary to call at your local flower shop and ask them to order a selection for you from their supplier.

Codiaeum 'Fred Sanders'

In recent years the poinsettia, *Euphorbia pulcherrima*, has become one of the most important of commercial greenhouse crops for December, and in recent years, too, the more modern varieties of poinsettia have become much easier for the mass producer of pot plants to handle. The breakthrough came with the introduction of *P. mikkelrochford* in 1967, its principal quality being that it was very much more tolerant of temperature variation and in its watering needs. Prior to the arrival of this plant it required the services of a highly skilled grower to keep them in good order, but nowadays they should be quite within the

Cauterizing a poinsettia cutting

scope of the person with a greenhouse that is adequately heated. This will mean having the ability to maintain temperatures of not less than 62°F (17°C) at least until the end of December, later if you want to have the greenhouse filled with poinsettias after Christmas. They may still be in flower by mid-summer!

An interest in poinsettias could well begin by acquiring a plant at Christmas—in which case it is kept until the leaves naturally yellow and drop off, followed by the disintegration of the coloured bract. The plant is then cut back to about 4in (10cm) of any older wood that may be there, or with younger plants, cut back to about 4in (10cm) from the top of the pot. Up to the time of complete loss of leaves the growing mix should be allowed to dry out gradually, and must be kept very much on the dry side until new growth is evident, when more water can be given. When the plant has produced a few tiny leaves much of the old growing mix is shaken off and the plant is potted into a slightly larger container using a mix with a good proportion of peat.

In warm, full light conditions growth will be quite rapid, and the growing tips of the plant can be pinched out when shoots are about 6in (15cm) long to encourage compact growth. In July cuttings can be taken—these should be about 5in (13cm) long, and the lower leaf should be removed before inserting cuttings individually in small pots in a heated propagator. Cuttings bleed a white sap when cut, and the severed end should be allowed to dry completely before it is pushed gently but firmly into the pure peat propagating medium. Cuttings will often flag alarmingly immediately after insertion, but recover in a day or two if they are regularly damped over with a fine rose, or put in a mist unit. Pot on when rooted into an open, peaty mixture using clay pots for preference, keeping the growing mix on the dry side until the plants have settled into the new medium. In good growing conditions (light and airy but not cold) plants will grow at a fair pace, and will need to have the growing tips of more vigorous shoots removed—or the top can be taken with three or four leaves attached and used as a cutting. Plants are then potted on as dictated by the amount of top growth that is produced—large plants look and do better in larger pots, and small plants likewise. Feed regularly when the plants are established, and ensure that they are grown in full light, with no artificial light, as extending the amount of light available in the twenty-four hours will delay or prevent the initiation of flower buds, and without these there will be no flowers with colourful red bracts surrounding them.

Besides the red coloured plants there are others with soft shades of pink and a fine one with creamy white bracts, also a variety with a mixture of white and pink that is rather insipid and not generally very well thought of. All the poinsettias that are grown commercially are treated with growth depressant chemicals to restrict the height of the plant, which makes it possible for them to offer

Gloxinia 'Saxon Court'

No pot plant display would be complete without an array of gloxinias plants of ideal size for the living room. Alas, the chemical is at present available only to the professional, so you will either have to get to know a professional grower and borrow some, or be content with plants that are much taller than those you can purchase from the flower shop.

As for a cut flower there is *Euphorbia fulgens* which has scarlet flowers in January/February, but it is a very troublesome plant to grow and one is so limited for space in the greenhouse that they are probably not worth handling—there is also a high temperature requirement.

Gesneriaceae

Although the foliage is unattractive, the flowers of the hot water plant, achimenes, are very colourful and a worthwhile addition to the greenhouse scene. Plants are grown from scaly tubers that are started into growth in February/March by placing them close together in seed boxes or small pots filled with moist peat. As they develop transfer them to 5in (13cm) pots, several to each pot, filled with J.I. No. 2 mix. Alternatively, they may be planted in hanging baskets, packing the baskets with young plants. As the plants die back naturally in the autumn water should be gradually withheld until the growing mix is quite dry—plants should then be stored in their pots in a warm place until the following February. New plants can be raised from seed sown in warm conditions in the spring, from spring-struck cuttings or by peeling scales from the tubers and planting them individually.

There can be few better plants for hanging baskets than the columneas, but they do require a bit of space once growth gets under way. In greenhouses with high sides they may also be utilized in pots on shelves along the wall, but only if there is ample clearance between them and the plants that are growing underneath. With three varieties you could have flowers from winter through to May—for winter flowering choose *C. gloriosa* which has brilliant red and yellow flowers; for spring flowering there are few better plants than the old-established *C.* × *banksii*, which has attractive blackish green foliage. Later still, *C. repens*, despite its tiny leaves that hang straight down from the basket or pot on slender stems, will provide a brilliant show of orange flowers that almost obliterate the foliage. Cuttings of all these root steadily in warm conditions, and they will grow freely in the warm, shaded house. Keep them well watered and fed, then on the dry side for several weeks prior to their natural flowering period in order to induce the maximum number of flowers from them. When plants become starved in their containers it is usually best to propagate fresh material and to dispose of older ones.

Gloxinias The many-coloured trumpet flowers of the gloxinias are a welcome sight in the greenhouse during the summer, and may be raised from seed sown in the warm propagator during the first two months of the year. When very fine surface-sown seed has produced leaves large enough to handle the young plants should be spaced out in seed boxes filled with J.I. No. 1 and allowed to establish before potting into shallow 5in (13cm) pots, care being taken to ensure that the plant is not potted too high in the compost. When tubers form on plants that have been potted too high there is a tendency for the plants to become 'swingers'—that is to say they are loose in their pots when plants have matured. When only a few plants are wanted they can be raised from tubers in much the same way as begonias, although the planting time can be delayed a few weeks. Shade plants from the sun, but maintain a buoyant atmosphere by regular damping down of the floor and staging and by airing the house whenever possible.

African violets Saintpaulias have become far and away the most popular plants in this family, mainly because of their desirability as houseplants, and the fact that they can be brought into flower at any time of the year without need for specialist equipment. However, they are not the easiest of plants to manage, as many a distraught housewife or greenhouse owner will tell you—professionals among the latter! Starting from the beginning—new plants are almost all raised from leaf cuttings taken at any time provided the conditions are right in respect of warmth, moisture and shading. Most important is the fact that cutting leaves should come from strong parent plants with healthy leaves—large, glossy and hairy ones! Start them in peat and sand and when clumps have developed to manageable sizes they should be gently teased apart and planted individually in boxes of J.I. No. 1 to which equal parts by volume of fresh peat have been added. Keep water off the leaves but ensure that the growing mix remains moist at this stage. Follow this stage when you have plants with leaves of reasonable size, by potting them into 3½in (9cm) pots using the same growing mix as before. Feed with weak liquid fertilizer once the roots are through to the sides of

The saintpaulia, better known as African violet

the pot and, when watering, use water with the chill taken off and at all times keep the water away from the leaves and flowers. However, having said all that, I must add that African violets are extremely difficult subjects to manage in a greenhouse that is filled with sundry other plants, no matter how well the house is managed or how skilful the operator.

They are very much a specialist crop that could well be handled in a section of the greenhouse that is divided off especially for growing these temperamental but beautiful plants. Scrupulously clean conditions are most essential, and good light is a must, although the greenhouse will have to be shaded in the summer. In winter it would be of considerable help if plants had the advantage of artificial lighting, sufficient for the plants to have some twelve hours of light each 24 hours—the light to be a mixture of natural and artificial.

Liliaceae

One of the easiest of all foliage plants to grow is *Chlorophytum comosum variegatum* (the spider plant) which does well in all sorts of conditions, although cold and extreme wetness would soon put paid to them. Easily grown from small plantlets that develop on the ends of long stalks of existing plants, they can go direct into the growing mixture, J.I. No. 2 being one of the many that is suitable. In small pots plants become starved and browning of leaf tips becomes a slight problem, but this is almost inevitable and the best thing to do is to remove the offending leaf when it is no longer pleasing to the eye.

More majestic, more demanding in respect of temperature and general care are the dracaenas, from which there is a wide selection. Of the taller plants that will need 8 to 10ft (2·5 to 3m) of headroom in due course, *Dracaena deremensis* and its variations are probably the best. Leaves are variegated grey, green and white and are carried on stout stems that will attain a height of some 8ft (2·5m), by which time it will have lost many of its lower leaves though still retaining its elegant appearance. Light shading of the glass and temperatures around 65°F (10°C) will be essential, plus regular feeding when the plants are estab-

Spider plants are easy to increase by layering

lished in their pots, and a watering programme that errs on the dry side. Plants grow at the rate of about 12in (30cm) each year, so there is ample time in which to enjoy the plant before it pushes the glass off! With narrow green leaves that are red margined, *D. marginata* is a much easier plant to grow, and will happily tolerate having its growing tip periodically removed to restrict the height. More compact is *D. godseffiana* 'Florida Beauty' which has gold and green speckled variegation, and makes an attractive compact bush if several young plants are put in the same pot. Depending on the size of the plants, J.I. No. 2 or 3 growing mix will suit them. Where possible use clay pots which will make plants of the taller type less top heavy.

Old indestructible *Sansevieria trifasciata Laurentii*, (mother-in-law's tongue) is arguably the toughest of all the foliage plants, and does seem to thrive on neglect—certainly doing very much better if it is watered once each month rather than once each day. To increase your collection, the plant should be knocked out of its pot and a sharp knife used to cut away with as much root as possible the young plants that in time form around the base of older plants. Plants may also be increased by cutting the leaves up into 3in (8cm) sections, but the resulting plant does not have the attractive yellow leaf margin of the parent. Keep these plants in full light, always on the dry side, and don't bother to feed them. The plant will break the pot in which it is growing when potting on becomes necessary, which is not very often. During the summer months older plants will sometimes oblige by producing pleasantly scented lime-green flowers.

Labiatae

Choose a good strain of seed, sow them in a propagating frame, with a temperature around 65°F (18°C) and you can have coleus in a dazzling array of colours throughout the summer months. As plants develop the poorer colours can be weeded out, and as flowers appear they should be removed as they do nothing for the plant. Use J.I. No. 2 when potting on, and once plants have been put into 5in (13cm) pots they should be sustained by regular feeding. Keep them moist and in good light and remove the growing point periodically to encourage a more bushy shape. There are many fine named varieties that you can purchase, but this will mean keeping stock plants over the winter at a minimum temperature of at least 50°F (10°C), which can be a costly business. With new strains of coleus it is much more sensible to raise new plants from seed annually—if

Sansevierias are easily increased from leaf cuttings

desired the best colours of these can be kept for propagating cuttings which root with little difficulty. Take the cuttings in August, so that young plants can be overwintered, and space-demanding older ones can be disposed of at the summer's end.

Malvaceae

Flowers of the many fine hybrid forms of *Hibiscus rosa-sinensis* are now available in a wide range of beautiful colours, but the snag is that they last only for a day. Some of the double flowered forms may hold for part of the second day, but the tendency is for them to open one day and be dead the next. There is a compensating factor, however, in that healthy plants produce an abundance of flowers and plants are seldom without some colour. Principal requirements are an abundance of good light, rich potting mix (J.I. No. 3 for example) and plenty of water and feeding while they are actively growing. In winter plants may be allowed to dry out and become dormant, in which case they will require an overwintering temperature in the region of 50°F (10°C). Alternatively, watering can continue, with the occasional application of weak fertilizer, and plants will retain their leaves and provide a reasonable number of flowers

during the winter, in which case they would need a temperature minimum of not less than 60°F (15°C). Healthy plants become quite large in time, but can be severely pruned in the spring—or they can be lightly pruned to shape if space is not a serious problem. This could also be a good time for selecting firm young cuttings with a view to propagation. Cuttings are difficult to root and will need temperatures in the region of 70°F (21°C) and the advantage of a closed propagating case or, better still, a mist propagating unit. Make

Coleus are easy to grow and make a bold splash of colour in the greenhouse

Hibiscus rosa-sinensis

Polythene tents make simple but successful greenhouse propagators

a clean cut, remove the lower leaf and place the cuttings around the outside edge of small pots that have been filled with a peat and sand mixture. Greenfly attacking young tip growth can be troublesome, so a careful watch must be kept.

Marantaceae

The marantas and calatheas are exotic foliage plants that are grown entirely for their colourful leaves, often with complicatedly patterned veins. Although *Maranta kerchoeviana* and *M. erythrophylla* may survive at lower temperatures, all the plants in this group will fare very much better if the temperature never drops below 60°F (15°C). To cope with these higher temperatures in the small greenhouse it is often wise to take cuttings of the older plants at the end of the summer and to overwinter these in a smaller and warmer section of the greenhouse—a home-made propagating type case for example—and to dispose of the older plants which require much more space. Firm cuttings with at least three leaves attached will not be difficult to root.

Anyone with ambition enough to consider growing such plants as *Calathea insignis*, *C. makoyana*, or *C. zebrina* must as a first essential be able to maintain at any time of the year a minimum temperature of not less than 60°F (15°C), and a higher minimum if possible. Besides warmth, plants will require quite heavy shade during the summer months, a very humid atmosphere but not over-wet growing mix, and the mix itself must be very open in the nature of a soilless mixture. Leaves of all the calatheas are much coveted by the flower arranger on account of their exotic colouring and unusual nature. Apply weak liquid fertilizer to established plants at regular intervals while they are in active growth.

Melastomaceae

Another testing plant even for the professional, but my goodness what an exotic beast you will have should you really get *Medinilla magnifica* to perform really well for you. My memories go back a long way, and encompass many shows and exhibitions around the country, but nothing seems to compare with a display of medinillas around a reflecting pool of water at a Chelsea Show some years back. Plants in time need fairly large pots (J.I. No. 3 mix) as they develop into large woody plants with coarse and comparatively unattractive leaves and will need regular feeding to keep them going. The growing mix must also be very free draining, so it is as well to add a little extra peat to the recommended compost to lighten it. Lightly shaded conditions suit them best, and they will require ample space in which to develop. Cuttings with one pair of firm leaves attached can be taken from non-flowering shoots at almost any time if a temperature of at least

Maranta leuconera thrives in warm humid conditions

Taking leaf bud cuttings of *Ficus tricolor*

65°F (18°C) can be maintained; one cutting to each 3½in (7cm) pot. So what is the attraction and advantage in keeping such a demanding plant in the greenhouse? It is in the superb pink, pendulous flowers that appear in late spring and go on throughout the summer months. Mature plants attain a maximum height of about 4ft (120cm) with a spread of about 3ft (90cm).

Moraceae

The fig family is extremely useful in providing many of the more stately plants for the large greenhouse and for office decoration, but they seem to have limited value as decorative plants for the smaller greenhouse—this is mentioned in spite of the fact that the most popular fig of all, the rubber plant, is sold in vast quantities for home decoration, to which they are better suited. In the greenhouse the majority of ficus plants are reasonably easy to grow, and frequently grow too well and take up very much more space than can be afforded. For most of them temperatures around 55°F (13°C) will be fine, with shade from strong sunlight, J.I. No. 3 mix and regular feeding once established with little or none being given in winter.

Strong growing plants such as *F. benjamina*, *F. robusta* (the rubber plant), *F. benghalensis* and *F. lyrata* (the fiddle-leaved fig) should have their roots confined to pots, with a watch being kept for roots coming through the bottom of the pot. There is often a tendency to plant these in the ground at one end of the greenhouse, but this is very unwise as plants are quite capable of pushing their heads through the glass, and they invariably become infested with pests of every description in the upper reaches of the garden greenhouse where they are difficult to detect. For the small house an attractive green-leaved plant is *Ficus pumila*, the creeping fig, which can provide a useful means of suppressing weeds if planted out under the staging—such plants can also be used for taking cuttings. The majority of ficus plants are best rooted in the winter when they are dormant—take firm cuttings and insert them in small pots filled with pure peat in a temperature of 65°F (18°C). It will greatly assist rooting if the bed in which the cutting pots are plunged can be at a temperature in the region of 70°F (21°C). Almost all cuttings of greenhouse plants would do better in warm peat beds.

Nyctaginaceae

The name suggests an unfortunate family of plants, to say the least, but if nothing else it contains that marvellous free flowering shrubby climber, the bougainvillea. Too difficult, too exotic—not at all. At Southport Show many years ago an old boy from Colwyn Bay was sold two flowering plants for his small greenhouse, and we (the sellers) thought 'there goes another bougainvillea to its last resting place'. But no, the same old boy was back three years later to go into great detail about how wonderfully well the plants had done, and were still doing—so you never can tell can you?

Full sun is most essential, a constant check for mealy bug must be carried out, and 10in (25cm) clay pots filled with J.I. No. 3 are best once plants have got established. Growing mix must drain freely, so the pot, which will most likely be standing on the ground, should be placed on a tile or brick to prevent the drainage hole becoming blocked. Potting on is done in the spring. Cuttings taken in the spring will not be difficult to root—even hard old pieces of previous years' growth seem to do perfectly well if done in a warm propagator. After flowering in the autumn allow the growing mix to dry off gradually, and keep bone dry from late October until new growth is evident in February when water should be gradually re-started. Also, at this time plants can be pruned back quite severely, and as new growth is produced it can be trained to canes, or to strained wires through the top of the greenhouse with reasonable space allowed between the plant and the top of the house. Minimum temperatures in winter of 50°F (10°C) will be ample, with no limit in summer provided the house is well aired and the growing mix moist.

The exotic-looking bougainvillea

Oleaceae

Fragrance is a worthwhile bonus in the small greenhouse, and one can have this in abundance in early spring by growing a few plants of *Jasminum polyanthum* which bears clusters of white flowers that are delicately tinged with pink in the bud stage. They can be planted out and allowed to climb against a wall if there is one, or be trained through the top of the house. Be warned, however: they are extremely invasive plants and are frequently less floriferous when allowed a free root run. Cuttings of firm material should be taken in the summer and several inserted in 3½in (9cm) pots, so that the potful of cuttings can have some of the cutting soil removed before plants are potted into 5in (13cm) pots using J.I. No. 2 mix. Plants will do better if left out of doors during the summer months, coming into the greenhouse in late September. Pot grown plants will need canes to support them, and frequent watering during the summer, less at other times.

Onagraceae

Everyone's favourite—few plants can be depended upon to give a better display in the greenhouse than the fuchsia, which flowers from March all the way through to October. Even in my small greenhouse the results can be quite spectacular, with plants in larger pots at the back of the staging and growth trained up the sides and then along the roof to the ridge, and shorter plants in front to complete the picture. Light shading is necessary and plenty of moisture on the floor and around the pots, and growing mix that is well fed and never allowed to dry out while the plants are actively growing. Following the flowering period plants can be tidied up, pushed together at one end of the house, and the soil allowed to dry out appreciably, though it should never be allowed to become bone dry. In spring they will tolerate hard pruning, but plants intended for climbing or those of standard habit must have their main stems left intact. Hard pruning of this kind may seem destructive, but plants quickly make new growth on which they will flower very much better.

Cuttings can be taken at almost any time when they are available, and given reasonable conditions present no problem. Pieces 3 to 4in (8 to 10cm) long are ideal, and should have all flowers and buds removed, also one or two lower leaves. Put several cuttings around the edge of 3½in (9cm) pots and put them in a shaded propagating frame. Pot on into rich potting mix as necessary, and remove the growing tips periodically of plants intended to grow as bushes, and allow plants intended as standards to run up to the desired height before removing the tip growth. As new growth develops at the top of the standard stem it should be allowed to produce several new leaves on each shoot before the tip is removed. Also, resist the temptation to remove the growth lower down the stem—instead it should be pinched back and left until such time as the top is well established when the stem, if desired, can be trimmed and left bare.

Because of poor light fuchsia plants make very poor indoor subjects, but are magnificent in the greenhouse or garden, be they in tubs on the terrace, planted in the border, in window boxes or offering a superb display as hanging basket subjects. A list of names may be thought necessary, but we all have our special favourites, and

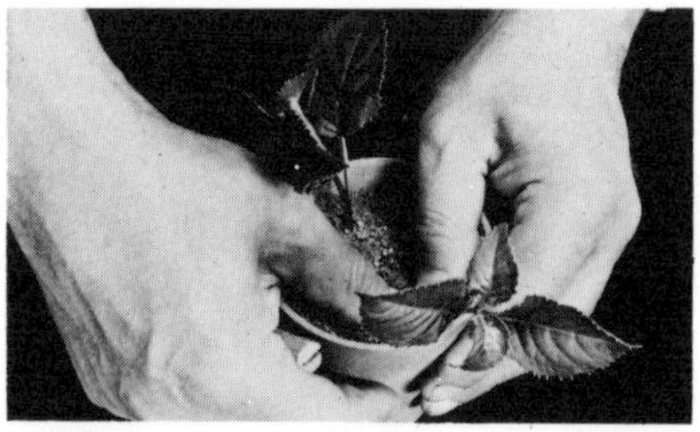

Taking fuchsia cuttings

the beginner could well start with a mixed batch of rooted cuttings, learn to grow them, then consult the specialist catalogue and just see what a wealth of colour and interest you can acquire at very little cost. But do not go mad on the new introductions—many of the very old established varieties will take a lot of beating.

Piperaceae

Here the principal interest for the greenhouse owner is in the peperomias which, though not particularly exciting, will provide small plants for the house during certain periods of the year when there is little else about. Provision of plants for indoor use becomes a necessity once the greenhouse contains a selection of plants, and many of the smaller plants can be very useful for helping to plant up mixed containers with foliage and flowering plants. There are several peperomias that one may obtain, but those most readily available are *P. caperata*, with rounded, very dark green crinkled leaves, *P. hederaefolia* with similarly rounded leaves that are a metalic grey in colour. There are a number of varieties with more fleshy leaves that are cream and green variegated: *P. magnoliaefolia*, *P. glabra* and *P. scandens*, all of which make interesting foil plants for other subjects in the greenhouse. Metallic grey leaves with a darker green striping are found on *P. sandersii*, which is propagated by the interesting method of cutting individual leaves into four equal sections and standing them upright in peat and sand with the severed edge just below soil level. All of them need soilless mix to do well, light shading and temperatures that do not fall much below 60°F (15°C).

Primulaceae

Cyclamen, in spite of the difficulty the average householder experiences in keeping them in the hot and airless conditions that are inevitable with central heating, are still among the most popular of all flowering pot plants. With seed grown plants we have seen many remarkable improvements in recent years, and with cyclamen there are now strains of seed that can be sown in the spring of the year to flower as mature plants well before Christmas of the same year. More traditionally, however, seed is sown in September/October of one year to flower the following Christmas, although some will flower before this time depending on the prevailing weather conditions. For best results, seed is sown evenly spaced about 1½in (4cm) apart in boxes filled with sowing mix. The seeds should be gently pressed into the mix and just covered. An oven-like temperature in the region of 70°F (21°C) is needed for efficient germination. When plants are large enough to be handled they should be carefully transferred to small thumb pots filled with J.I. No. 1 and allowed to establish in a temperature of about 60°F (15°C) before potting them into 3½in (9cm) pots of J.I. No. 2. Final potting is into 5in (13cm) pots using the same growing mix. While growing on a temperature of 55°F (13°C) is ideal, and light shading with lots of air about the plants will be essential. In summer (to save space for the fuchsias!) plants can spend their time in a cool frame out of doors, with a careful watch being kept for greenfly, and in particular for botrytis fungus showing itself between the crowded leaf stalks. At all times plants will require frequent handling to ensure that all dead and dying leaves are removed, also premature flowers which should be pulled clean away from the corm with a gentle tug—likewise no part of dead leaves should be left, possibly to rot the remainder of the plant.

New plants from fresh seed each year are the best bet if you want quality plants, but corms can be kept from one year to the next by allowing plants to die naturally and then keeping the soil almost dry by placing the plant pot on its side under the greenhouse staging until such time as new growth appears when watering can begin. When a reasonable amount of growth has been made the plant can be taken from its pot and the old soil removed before repotting the corm in fresh J.I. No. 2 and starting the growing process all over again. Remember that a buoyant, airy atmosphere is essential and frequent cleaning over of plants to ensure that they are free from pests and diseases. Cyclamen are an example of plants that are difficult to combine with other subjects on account of the special cool conditions that they require.

Following the blaze of December colour provided by the poinsettias it comes as a very welcome change to see the first *Primula malacoides* with their soft, attractive leaves and whorls of tiering flowers in many lovely colours. Seeds of these are sown in early June in a temperature of 60°F (15°C), with the very fine seed needing only a sprinkling of sand to cover it. Prick off into seedboxes as soon as the young plants are able to be handled, and pot on into 3½in (9cm) pots, using J.I. No. 2, when firm little plants have developed. If larger plants are wanted, then plants can be

Primula x *kewensis*

Primula malacoides, one of the most popular members of its family potted on when ready into 5in (13cm) pots using the same mix. Like the cyclamen they will do fine in the garden frame during the summer months, care being taken to ensure that the frame is shaded from strong sunlight, and to see that it is well aired on hotter days. Established plants will need regular feeding, and growing mix should be kept moist, although water should be kept off leaves and flowers.

Primula obconica is another excellent plant that is almost permanently flowering once it has become established, and needs very much the same treatment as the plant mentioned above, with the exception that the seed should be sown a couple of months earlier in the year. Anyone with sensitive skin would be well advised to think twice about growing primulas in the greenhouse—if skin irritation is experienced the primulas should immediately be suspected as being the cause of your discomfort.

Polypodiaceae

For the greenhouse that is set out with maximum display effect in mind a selection of the many ferns that are available would seem to be almost indispensable, in particular the maidenhairs (*Adiantum capillus hueneris*) with their soft green delicate foliage. Shade is essential, and many of them will be quite content to make a home underneath the staging where they will need little more than a damp over as you are passing with the watering can. For the warmer house with a temperature maintained at not less than 60°F (15°C) the pale green leaves formed in the manner of a shuttlecock by *Asplenium nidus avis*, the bird's nest fern, will, as it ages, become a very fine feature plant. Growing mix should be of a peaty nature and must be kept moist. Scale insects can become a problem if not detected—keep them under control by wiping off the plants with a sponge that has been soaked in malathion solution.

Ferns are becoming increasingly popular

The stag's horn fern, *Platycerium bifurcatum*, is another plant that is likely to suffer scale attack, but will also provide a major feature in the greenhouse if several young plants are put in a hanging basket and suspended from the ridge. Alternatively, the root ball can be wrapped in a thick layer of sphagnum moss which in turn can be attached to a section of cork bark around which the anchor roots of the plants will grow and in time completely enclose the bark support. The principal fronds of the plants will grow away from the bark and look for all the world like a stag's antlers, hence the common name.

Plants can be increased by removing small plantlets from around the parent plant when they are large enough, and planting them in small pots filled with a very peaty mixture. Possibly the finest display plant of all is *Nephrolepis* with large green fronds that are so impressive when seen as full hanging baskets, or in large pots placed on top of pedestals in the conservatory or indoors. Growing mix must be well watered and never allowed to dry out, and plants should not be subjected to direct sunlight.

Ferns seemed to go through a very dull period, but now appear to be regaining in popularity, with the result that many more commercial establishments are growing them again. For the amateur grower this may not appear very interesting, but it is only in this way that plants become more generally available. Due to the wide diversity of requirements, it is wise when purchasing ferns of any kind to enquire about the growing conditions, in particular the minimum temperature that is needed. Getting stock in the first place, and subsequent propagation of plants from spores can be difficult, but *Platycerium bifurcatum*, *Nephrolepis* and *Adiantums* can simply be increased by carefully dividing mature plants in spring.

Rutaceae

Visions of the greenhouse being filled with exotic fruits may well rest in the imagination of the ambitious beginner with the greenhouse. But let it be said that few of the varieties mentioned in the older books on the subject mention heights of less than 10ft (3m), and in the small greenhouse that is just not realistic. Anyway, most of the citrus plants

Ferns in outline against a window

that you may acquire or even grow from your own seed germinated in high temperature will prove to be ugly old things taking up too much space, and will never fruit anyway. So why mention the plants? Because the dwarf growing *Citrus mitis* (calamondin orange) is a beautiful decorative plant with glossy leaves, compact habit and fruits that set fairly readily each year. It has glossy foliage, needs maximum sun and light and free watering in spring and summer. Heavily scented white flowers are at their most abundant in September and not all of them will set fruit by any means, but we have known plants in 10in (25cm) pots to be carrying as many as 200 fruits during the summer, and the plant less than 4ft (120cm) from the floor to the topmost leaf.

Plants should be gradually potted on when they have filled their existing pots until they are in 10in (25cm) pots; thereafter they can be sustained by regular feeding with a balanced fertilizer while they are actively growing. The fruit is bitter, though edible, but is grown principally for its decorative value. Plants are raised from seed or cuttings, but they are seldom as good as the specially grafted bought plants.

Rubiaceae

A prominent houseplant grower once said that if a plant had naturally glossy leaves it was well on the way to being accepted by the amateur for indoor decoration. Although one would dread the thought of trying to grow *Gardenia jasminoides* in the average living room, there is little doubt that it has attractive glossy leaves and, as an added bonus, it has heavily scented double white flowers that could quite well take your breath away.

They are lime-hating plants, so any growing

mix that is used must be free of chalk and, if mixing John Innes, do a little juggling with the recipe—omit the chalk and reverse the amount of peat and loam, so that a much more peaty mixture results. (Where a peaty mixture is advised, mixing the peat and loam in reverse is a simple way of arriving at a good medium).

Minimum temperatures of not less than 55°F (13°C) should be maintained, and established plants should be fed regularly, at least once each week, while plants are producing new leaves. Cuttings with a heel of older wood can be rooted in early spring in a heated propagating case, and should have growing tips pinched out once they are established in their first 3½in (9cm) size pots. Chlorotic discolouration of leaves is a frequent problem that raises many questions—the condition is caused by iron deficiency and can be rectified by watering plants with sequestrated iron.

Scrophulariaceae

Calceolarias are among the brightest of greenhouse summer flowering plants, and to spread the display over April, May and June, seed should be sown in three small batches between August and October of the previous year. For the best plants,

Brunfelsia calcyina, a member of the Solanacea family, fades in colour from purple to white

get F_1 seed. The fine seed should be sown in pans filled with sifted sowing mix and need not be covered. When large enough to be handled they should go into 2in (5cm) pots, or peat pots which will save the plants being checked at the next potting as the peat pot is also potted into the larger container. From the small pots they can go into their final 5in (3cm) pots, using J.I. No. 2 mix. Grow them through the winter in a temperature midway between 45 and 50°F (7 and 10°C) and maintain an airy atmosphere in the house. As plants begin to bud up they should be fed weekly with a liquid fertilizer.

Solanaceae

The Christmas cherry, *Solanum capsicastrum*, provides a colourful display of orange berries in December—provided all goes well!

Solanum capsicastrum, the Christmas cherry

Sow seed in February, and prick off and pot plants as they become large enough, but be sure to maintain temperatures at around 50°F (10°C) in order to keep plants on the move. Growth should be pinched to about five breaks in early May, and during May pinch out the growing tips to produce neatly shaped plants. Plants may be stood out of doors during the summer months where they can enjoy full sun, but it is important that they should not dry out. Plants should also be lifted occasionally to remove any roots that may be growing through the bottom of the pot, as it will be too much of a shock to the plant if this is done when they are picked up to go into the greenhouse during September. From the time they are taken in less water is required, but it is essential that plants have the lightest possible conditions. Regular feeding with a liquid fertilizer is also important, particularly after the berries have set.

Urticaceae

Among the pileas there are a number of compact and attractive varieties that could well add to the interest in the greenhouse where growing the widest possible selection of plants is an important consideration. All are low growing and easily propagated from cuttings taken at almost any time of the year in reasonably warm conditions. Several cuttings should go into small pots of peaty compost and the tips must be removed once they begin to produce new leaves, otherwise they become long and straggly. Tired old plants are best disposed of and replaced with fresh young plants that will be much more attractive. *Pilea cadienei* 'Nana', aluminium plant, is probably the best known and does well in rich growing mix in the lightly shaded greenhouse where the temperature does not drop much below 55°F (13°C). Growing mix must be kept moist, but avoid wet and dank conditions in the greenhouse.

A half wall greenhouse is excellent for growing pot plants

6 Alpines

Plants that are more usually associated with the rock garden would seem to be some way removed from the greenhouse in the accepted sense. But one of my great pleasures is to visit the R.H.S. Gardens at Wisley in Surrey and make my way slowly up through the rock garden from the lower side. At the top there is a greenhouse surrounded by sundry cold frames, and a grand selection of small plants growing in sink gardens—the sort of scene that could well be copied on a smaller scale in the average garden. The greenhouse is quite conventional, positively modest by many standards, and about 30 × 12ft (9 × 3·6m) in area. The great attraction of the house is its ever-changing selection of alpines, many very rare and others not so.

Many of the alpine plants are very small, so it is wise to build staging of reasonable height, about 4ft (120cm) from the ground, so that the plants can be better appreciated, and be nearer the glass where they may enjoy the maximum amount of light. Although the greenhouse is not normally shaded it could, on very hot days, be a benefit to have some form of matting to prevent the inside of the house becoming insufferably hot. Split bamboo laced together provides an excellent form of portable shading for this purpose—the matting can be dual purpose in that it may be used during the winter to cover the glass when the weather is very severe. Also, when the weather is very severe in winter many of the plants will fare better if their pots are plunged to their rims in peat. On the whole, however, free drainage for alpine plants growing in pots, or pans, is of paramount importance. Therefore it is advisable to cover the staging with a coarse grade of gravel and to ensure that all pots are amply provided with crocks, and to prepare growing mix that is not likely to mat together and prevent air getting into the soil.

One of the principal advantages of this type of greenhouse interest is that there is no necessity to heat the house, and there are none of those imperative jobs that seem to be forever cropping up when more conventional plants are being grown. This is not to say that there is nothing to do—it would be strange indeed to find the man with a greenhouse who had nothing to do! If the greenhouse with alpines is to be some sort of show place it will be essential to have a fairly large cold frame that is run in conjunction with the greenhouse—the reason being that as interesting plants come into flower they can be transferred from the frame to the greenhouse, and plants that have passed their best can be removed to the frame. When setting up the interior of the house with plants the aim is not to crowd in as many as one possibly can—plants will look better and grow better if they all have ample space. Although deeper pots may be preferable as far as the root

A view into a well-kept alpine house

Adenium obesum can be grown in the alpine house

development of plants goes, almost all of them will be more appealing to the eye if they are in shallow pans made of natural material.

The slower growing types of plants are best, and as slower plants are usually in the same size pots for longer periods it is good practice to make a thorough job of the potting operation. To prevent worms getting into the pots a piece of perforated zinc or plastic should be placed over the drainage hole and a liberal layer of crocks should then be put in the bottom of the pot. For the general run of alpines in pots John Innes No. 1 mix can be used, but one should add enough grit and sharp sand to give it a gritty feel when it is rubbed through the hands. As with other forms of greenhouse gardening you will adapt and experiment with other mixes until that special mix of your own has been reached. For ericacious plants, small azaleas and camellias, something akin to the following would be advisable; one part peat, one part leafmould and half part sand, and no fertilizer. Chippings are frequently used to cover the growing mix on top of the pot and present a more pleasing appearance but, unless you are able to detect wet from dry by the ring of the pot when it is tapped, this practice

Chamaecyparis obtusa is an easy alpine

Juniperus squamata Mayerii will do well in the alpine house

The Venus fly trap is a fascinating alpine to grow

can make it difficult to tell whether the mix in the pot is wet or dry.

Damp and continually wet conditions are one of the main reasons for the loss of what may be termed more delicate alpine plants when they are planted out in the garden, so damp and wet are the conditions to avoid in the alpine house. For many of the plants it is particularly damaging for the foliage to be watered over when there is little chance of it drying out. The aim in the greenhouse should be light and airy conditions with ventilators and doors open on almost every day of the year. For some of the shade loving plants it would not be amiss to provide a shaded corner where they would get some protection from the sun.

A good question could be, 'What to grow?'. And the answer is that there is a tremendous range of plants but, as already mentioned, the emphasis must be on slower growing subjects. An excellent start could be made with a selection of dwarf conifers, which in time will provide an ideal background for other subjects. A selection could be made from the following:

Conifers All conifers will in time become quite large, and so it is important to choose the very slow-growing ones so that they can have a long life in the alpine house. *Picea glauca* and *P. abies* both have attractive cones, and conifers which do not bear cones at all include the juniper and yew families which carry fleshy berries instead.

It may be a good idea to plant dwarf conifers in your alpine house in groups; they are often effective this way, and they also contrast well with heathers if these are planted near them.

Cyclamen The miniature hardy cyclamen are all ideal for the alpine greenhouse, and can be had in flower for many months of the year; *C. orbiculatum* flowers early in the year and is followed in March/April by *C. repandum*, and later in the year there is *C. europaeum* followed into the winter by the pink and white colours of *C. neapolitanum*.

Primulas There are also numerous smaller primulas that are almost impossible to manage out of doors but can be encouraged to do very much better in the greenhouse—in the shaded section where they can be accompanied by a few of the less vigorous hardy ferns. The latter are in short supply but there are one or two nurseries stocking them, though it is often a case of accepting what is available rather than getting what you actually want.

Saxifrages The neat hummocks of silver foliage formed by the encrusted saxifrages make them particularly fine plants for growing in shallow pans, and they will also oblige with splendid flowers. Establishing a collection of these is not difficult as they propagate very readily from almost any small piece of the plant—to have more instant plants one can remove small sections of older plants with a trowel or spoon and plant them up to form neat rosettes in very little time. The green or mossy saxifrages can also be used, but tend to outgrow their pots much more rapidly.

Sempervivums Also neat plants of particular interest are the sempervivums (house leeks) which are very easy to care for and are available in a wide range of varieties. These could well be the principal interest of anyone wishing to specialize. They must have full light if the rosettes are to retain their compact shape, and it is interesting to plant several rosettes in a larger pan with a piece of rock for the plants to grow around and over in time. *Sempervivum arachnoideum* has the added attraction of being covered in fine hairs that resemble cobwebs. All the houseleeks propagate very simply by removing individual rosettes and potting them individually in small containers.

Dianthus A selection from the many dwarf dianthus, such as *D. mars* would provide attractive foliage and colourful flowers during the summer. Many of the more compact campanulas will also offer additional colour when one first sets up the greenhouse, but thereafter the tendency usually is to think of the campanulas as being rather ordinary and to favour something that is more delicate and more challenging.

There is a vast range of plants to choose from, and the cold greenhouse filled with alpines really can become an absorbing interest, and one is spared the cost and the problems that are frequently associated with the heated house.

Nicotiana, tobacco plant. An attractive half-hardy annual which is easily raised under glass

7 Cut Flowers and Annuals

For those who recall the mountains of blazingly colourful plants displayed at Chelsea Flower Show by Carters and Suttons there is little need to say what value can be obtained from a few packets of seed. The withdrawal of these two companies spelt the end of an era for Chelsea, and one wonders what sort of fantastic plants they would be able to produce now with the advantage of F_1 hybrid seed. In a foolish moment last year I purchased F_1 seed of *Ageratum* 'Blue chip', and the incredible growth that developed made a mockery of their supposed use as edging plants, but it did indicate that by spending a little extra on the best seed one can surely reap the benefits—unless it happens to be an edging plant that gets out of hand!

For the owner of the garden greenhouse however, it is important that the best results possible should be achieved from the limited space that is available and, if seed is expensive, it may be wise to share the cost with another greenhouse owner. With costly seed there may only be ten seeds in the packet, in which case you can have four plants each—if you get 80% germination! As seed packets get slimmer and slimmer it could be good sense to enquire from the retailer the approximate number of seed that you can expect to find in each packet. A perplexed colleague approached me recently with a packet which contained precisely six very minute seeds—one piece of advice on the back of the packet clearly stated 'Sow thinly'!

Given controlled greenhouse conditions and a little expertise the very ordinary bedding plants, antirrhinum for example, can take on a completely new appearance. The F_1 impatiens, Busy Lizzies, are quite superb plants in hanging baskets or pots, and F_1 geraniums, though expensive, will save you the cost of overwintering stock plants. And from seed each year can there be a better climbing plant for the unheated greenhouse than *Ipomoea* 'Heavenly blue', the morning glory with trumpet-shaped flowers that last for only one day, but can be guaranteed to produce fresh flowers every day for week after week. And what greenhouse owner could be without *Lobelia pendula*, either 'Blue cascade' or 'Sapphire', to provide the finishing touch to hanging baskets for the greenhouse?

Capsicum The pepper plant bears an abundance of ornamental fruits above dark green foliage, and is raised from seed sown in April and grown on in smaller pots, up to 4in (10cm) size and offers an additional interest and splash of colour in the greenhouse that is kept for ornamental purposes. Good light, adequate moisture and feeding are essential requirements. Capsicums may also be grown as vegetables but, unless required for pickling, those with milder flavour should be chosen, and mature fruits should be harvested before they fully ripen.

Carnations The perpetual flowering carnations are useful for providing a limited number of flowers throughout the year, but are not so very perpetual as they will have to be changed every

A seedbox hole-maker

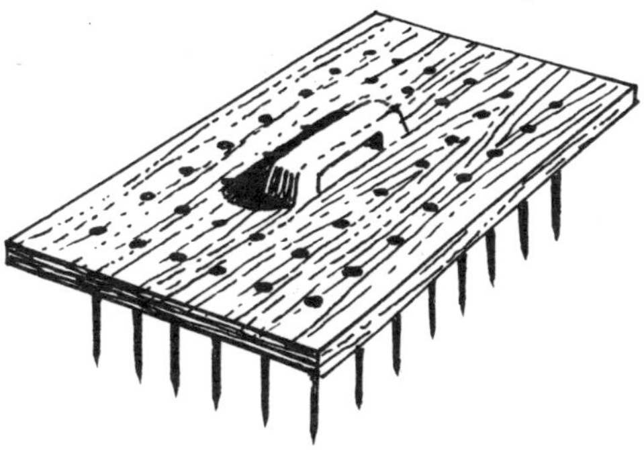

Carnations always give pleasure to the keen gardener

Carnation cuttings

third year or so. You can start by purchasing rooted young plants for potting and growing on, or by acquiring unrooted cuttings about 4in (10cm) long and rooting them in sandy compost in a warm propagating case, or you can make a start with good quality seed and use the best plants so raised for propagating fresh stock.

As plants fill their existing pots with roots they should be gradually potted on into larger containers if you intend keeping them in pots, or they can be planted in prepared beds in the greenhouse once they have filled their first small pots with roots. Few smaller greenhouses will, however, be suitable for permanent beds of carnation plants as there are always so many other things in need of the valuable space. Plants in pots are so much more adaptable, and can stand in a sheltered spot out of doors during the summer months when the tomatoes take over! Keep plants lightly shaded in very hot periods, well watered when in active growth and fed with a fertilizer containing a high proportion of potash. (The latter information applies to almost all plants that are being grown principally for their flowers). To promote more bushy habit young plants should have their tops pinched out when they are about 15in (38cm) tall, and as they develop subsequent side growths they should have their tips removed.

Most of the more usual greenhouse pests will make a home on carnations and therefore precautions should be taken against red spider, greenfly and thrips, while the raised brown spots indicative of rust should be treated with lime sulphur. Alas, there is no cure for plants that are affected by virus so it is advisable to destroy them by burning.

Disbudding carnations for an improved display

Layering a carnation. All that need be done is to make a slight slit in the stem just below the node, insert it in a handful of sand in the soil, firm it and bend it upwards. The layers will be ready for planting on in the following season

Chrysanthemum The dedicated chrysanthemum grower in the hobby sense is quite a different breed from the rest of us, as almost everything he or she does is centered around chrysanthemums and one could not possibly imagine the dedicated enthusiast taking any advice from the comparatively simple information that will be offered here. Never mind, we may be able to set someone off on the wondrous journey through the many facets of chrysanth growing that is cloaked in almost Masonic secrecy!

Your first contact may well be through the purchase of a compact chrysanthemum plant in a 5in (13cm) pot from the local greengrocer. Going into detail on the complicated production of these seemingly simple plants would be pointless here as it is an extremely involved operation that would be almost impossible to emulate in your green-

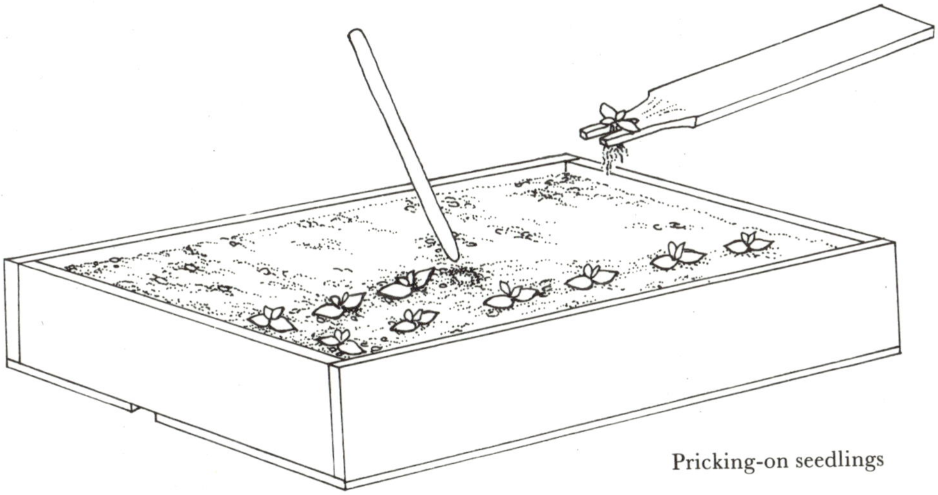

Pricking-on seedlings

Chrysanthemum 'Sunrise'

Disbudding chrysanthemums

house. Briefly, however, five cuttings stopped at 4in (10cm) are put around the outside edge of 5in (13cm) pots which will in time provide plants about 15in (38cm) tall with some 20 blooms giving an even spread of colour. Plants are restricted to the unnatural height of 15 to 18in (38 to 45cm) by treating them with carefully measured doses of growth retarding chemicals, the effects of which the plants outgrow in time. Plants are available every day of the year, and not only during the latter part of the year which is the natural time for chrysanthemums. This is achieved by subjecting, through covering with black polythene, the plants to controlled amounts of daylight that are the same as conditions prevailing at the plants natural flowering time. (Poinsettias can be treated the same way.) Once plants have flowered they can be grown on in normal conditions. Having finished flowering indoors, the usual procedure is to plant them in the garden where they will revert to their normal cycle of growth and flowering.

To see the chrysanthemum enthusiast prepare and arrange his plants on the show bench is to witness something that approaches devotion as nothing is left to chance. Every flower comes packed and individually spaced in a transit case, and every petal is carefully arranged with nothing left to chance, and there are always surreptitious glances along the line to see what wonder of nature the next man has managed to produce. And why not—the blooms on the show bench are the result of some twelve months of undivided attention, endless time, skill and not a little tender loving care.

The previous year old plants would have been cut down after flowering and the very best of the stools shaken free of soil before they were carefully placed in deepish boxes to overwinter with a little fresh growing mix around the stools. In a cool, light place fresh growth will develop around the base of the old stem, and in January or February of the following year the firmest of these shoots, 3 to 4in (8 to 10cm) long, will have been removed with a sharp knife and inserted in sandy compost, several in small pots or in regimental lines in sandy compost in the propagating bed at a steady temperature of 45°F (16°C).

Following rooting, plants would be progressively potted on into larger containers, using something similar to John Innes No. 1 mix to start with, and No. 3 by the time the plant is in its final 10in (25cm) pot—besides the J.I. mixes there would also be many other magical potions of which you would only learn the ingredients on entering the magic circle of chrysanthemum enthusiasts. Plants are kept in good light and moved to the garden when weather is more open and placed on a bed of ashes, or gravel with reasonable space between pots and rows of pots. A stout post driven in at either end of each row can be used for straining a wire along the row which should be about 4ft (120cm) above the plants. By now plants will have been staked and the tops of the 4ft (120cm) stakes can be secured to the wire to prevent wind damage. Watering and feeding will be of paramount importance while plants are out of doors.

Towards the end of September they are taken back into the light and airy greenhouse that is capable of maintaining a temperature of not less than 45°F (7°C).

By now the experienced man will be shaking his head and thinking, 'But what about all the stopping, disbudding and such like that should have been done?'.

And this writer would say that he is not so daft as to go into such detail here, otherwise we should never get off the subject. Also, there are so many varieties and types of chrysanthemums and an apparently endless supply of new varieties, it is very much better on purchasing or acquiring your plants to get the relevant information concerning their treatment from the supplier. Some varieties have to be stopped by removing the growing tip in order to induce side growths, while others produce side growths quite naturally.

When stopped, plants will produce side growths which should be reduced to some six per plant, which are allowed to grow on and produce terminal flowers. If larger blooms are required it is necessary to remove all buds but the topmost as they appear. If large flowers are not important the topmost cluster of blooms should be left to provide a spray of smaller blooms. In recent years the American spray chrysanthemum has surely become the world's most popular cut flower, and is

A chrysanthemum growing in an expanded Jiffy pot

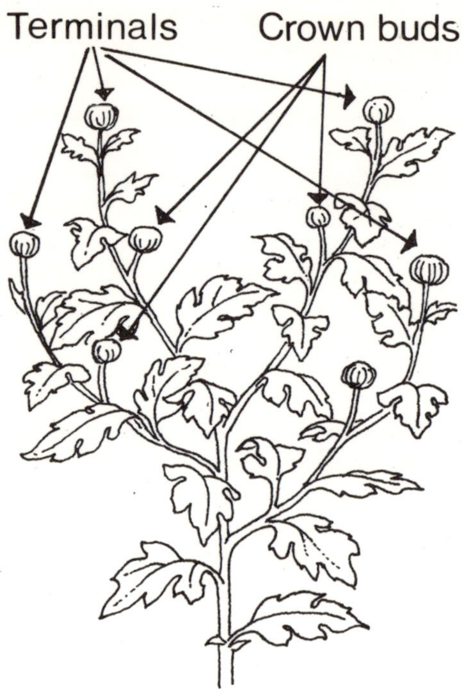

A chrysanthemum, showing terminals and crown buds

available all-the-year-round. These plants are grown in large, airy greenhouses, the rooted cuttings being planted directly into prepared beds on the floor of the greenhouse at a spacing of 7in (18cm) in each direction.

Most commercial growers purchase fresh rooted cuttings from specialist propagators for each of their various growing exercises with chrysanthemums, so ensuring that they are working with vigorous young stock with each new crop. Chrysanthemums are susceptible to many fatal virus and fungal diseases, and therefore it is wise to acquire new stock from a reliable source, and not to persevere with old stock that has clearly seen better days.

Brown rust on chrysanthemum plants has always been something of a problem, but never a very serious one. However, by way of Japan and Holland in recent years the increase in the incidence of white rust has become a major problem. So much so that even private individuals are advised to contact their local office of the Ministry of Agriculture and Fisheries if they suspect that their plants are affected by white rust. The first symptoms of white rust are pale yellow spots, up to 4mm in diameter, on the upper surfaces of the leaves. The centres of the spots eventually turn brown and on their undersides prominent waxy pustules develop. The pustules

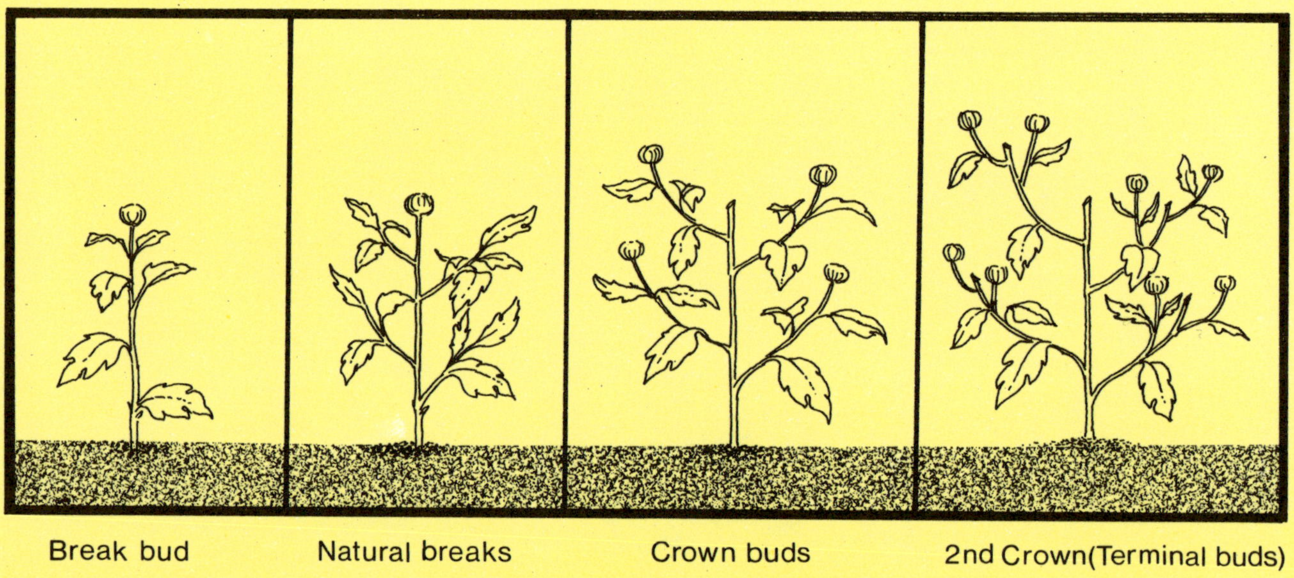

are initially oatmeal or pinkish, but in time they lose their waxy appearance and assume the characteristic white coloration. At the time of writing the commercial grower is being advised to use chemicals that will reduce the infection or spread of the white rust but the general concern that is being shown clearly indicates that there is no cure. Should you suspect white rust, affected plants should be segregated, or carefully handled before burning in an incinerator. Carefully handled, because the spores of the fungus can be transmitted through the air or on clothing, so it may be wise to slip a polythene sack over the plant before it is moved with the thought in mind that the sack and plant should go on the fire. As mentioned above, spores can be carried on ones clothing, so the chrysanthemum grower should think twice about entertaining any colleague who may have come into contact with plants affected by white rust. The wisest precaution however is to seek advice, and certainly to inform the local office of the Ministry of Agriculture if your suspicions are aroused.

Freesias In recent years we have seen numerous improvements in the size, length of stem and colour of freesia flowers—many of them now being semi-double. The beautifully clear colours of these delicate flowers on wiry stems is further enhanced by their room-filling scent. In spite of all these wonderful qualities freesias only require high temperatures when seed is being germinated, thereafter they can be grown on at temperatures around 45°F (7°C). My memories go back a long way with these plants—to the days of the feared and respected Phil Ellis who was so demanding and particular about everything he did in connection with the growing of plants. His freesia seed was always mixed in with clean moist peat in an equally clean bucket and placed in a greenhouse with temperatures maintained at about 70°F (21°C) to germinate. This method overcame the problem of erratic germination, as the peat, once the first seed had germinated, was carefully tipped out at regular intervals and the sprouted seedlings removed and pricked out into deep boxes.

Freesias resent root disturbance, so the deep boxes filled with John Innes No. 2 mix were in fact the containers in which the plants would eventually flower. Seed can be started at any time early in the year, and the earlier ones should be in time for December flowering. Once in boxes, or large pots, the temperature can be gradually lowered until plants are being maintained at around 45°F (7°C), and during the summer freesia plants will do perfectly well in a light, airy frame out of doors, coming in about the end of September.

Although one may be tempted to begin by purchasing corms (which seed plants will in time develop) these are frequently disappointing, unless one is able to acquire large bulbs. Phil Ellis always threw away his corms and made a fresh start with seed each year! He knew full well that they produced a better and more reliable crop. But if you must have corms, then plant ten of them in a 7in (18cm) pot filled with J.I. No. 2 mix in the month of August and place the pots in a cold frame under a covering of peat—treated in much the same way as spring bulbs being grown in pots. Once established, towards the end of September, the plants can be taken to the greenhouse to grow on.

When foliage begins to die down naturally water should be gradually withheld until such time as the growing mix is quite dry when plants in their boxes or pots should be stored in a warm and dry place until they are planted in fresh mix and started into growth in August.

Annuals

One of the great benefits of a greenhouse in the garden is in the ability to produce all sorts of plants and flowers ahead of their natural flowering time out of doors. And it need not be terribly exotic flowers—you can experiment with all sorts of humble garden annuals and have a greenhouse full of colour at very little cost. It is not for the dedicated greenhouse man, but cost could be a consideration that will prompt the greenhouse owner to leave the greenhouse empty during the more costly winter months and to start again in the spring. Or you could cut costs by having a smaller greenhouse that is heated and used for housing more valuable stock over the winter, so that cuttings, or whatever, can be taken in the spring to fill the greenhouse and the smaller house. Alternatively, use a heated frame to overwinter your stock of fuchsias and any similar plants and the running costs will be even further reduced.

Some of the annuals that can be grown as pot plants will give considerable pleasure at very little cost. The compact celosias (cockscombs) in their many brilliant colours will provide attractive plants at very little cost. Seed is sown in March and grown on in similar temperature in the region of 65°F (18°C)—final pots should not be more than 5in (13cm) in diameter, as larger would be out of proportion for these short and compact plants. Keep the growing mix moist and

You can raise half hardy annuals such as these African marigolds to go into the garden later

Zinnias can be raised under glass for summer planting

Verbenas ready for transfer to the garden

feed well once established in their final pots.

Where something taller, around 30in (75cm), is required you will find clarkias little trouble in the greenhouse that is light and airy. Pinch out the tips of young plants to encourage more bushy growth, and pot on into slightly larger pots using J.I. No. 2 as necessary, but avoid putting plants into anything larger than containers 7in (18cm) in diameter. If only for their fragrance one should sow seed of *Reseda odorata* (mignonette); sow in August and keep fairly dry over winter for plants to flower early in the year, and sow in spring for flowers in early autumn. Another favourite plant for its fragrance is the tobacco plant *Nicotiana*, seed of which should be sown in the spring, to grow on and eventually be potted into 7in (18cm) pots. Salpiglossis is another of the taller annuals available in many colours that will provide an excellent background plant for the greenhouse that offers reasonable height between staging and

An aluminium garden frame with a top that can be slid sideways or hinged upwards

the glass—one good reason for selecting a house with higher side walls.

We began this section by mentioning the grand Chelsea exhibits, and end by adding that few of the displays by the seed firms would have been complete without their high banks of dazzling *Schizanthus*—also given the appropriate common name of butterfly flower and poor man's orchid. Plants require cool conditions and seed can be sown at varying times—August/September of one year to flower in the spring of the following year, or in the spring to flower around September of the same year. Pot plants on, using J.I. No. 2 mix as plants fill their existing pots with roots—quite spectacular plants will result if they are carefully handled and progressively potted on. Nip out the tips when about 6in (15cm) high, and when they are reasonably tall four stakes should be put in at intervals around the outside edge of the pot to support the plant as it increases in height. Feed them well once established in their pots, and keep a watchful eye for the usual greenhouse pests of greenfly and such like.

Greenhouse plants can provide much larger heads for cutting than outdoor flowers

8 Fruit and Vegetables

In the grand orangeries of our Victorian forebears it was possible and quite practical to produce all sorts of exotic fruits for the table, especially so if the plants could be trained to a wall forming the back of the conservatory, or orangery. And it ought to be perfectly possible for the owner of the smaller greenhouse to appear in the kitchen with oranges, figs, apricots and such like plucked from his or her own trees. But from a practical standpoint it really is not viable, as the most precious commodity in any small greenhouse is space, and most of the exotic fruits will require a deal of that and they will not be very prolific. Purchasing the fruit from the greengrocer will be a good deal less expensive than the years of time and cost that will go into growing your own!

However, that is not to say that you cannot grow your own tomatoes, cucumbers, melons, grapes, strawberries, carrots, turnips, or even early forced rhubarb. The principal difficulty when growing any sort of food crop in the small greenhouse is that the owner of the small greenhouse almost invariably has an insatiable desire to collect all the plants he possibly can, and the more varied and more weird the collection the better he seems to like it. How do I know?—I'm one of them! The commercial grower depending on his tomato crop for his living would be horrified

Zingiber officinale, from which ginger is made; worth growing for its looks if not for eating

Aubergines are an interesting and tasty vegetable to grow in the greenhouse

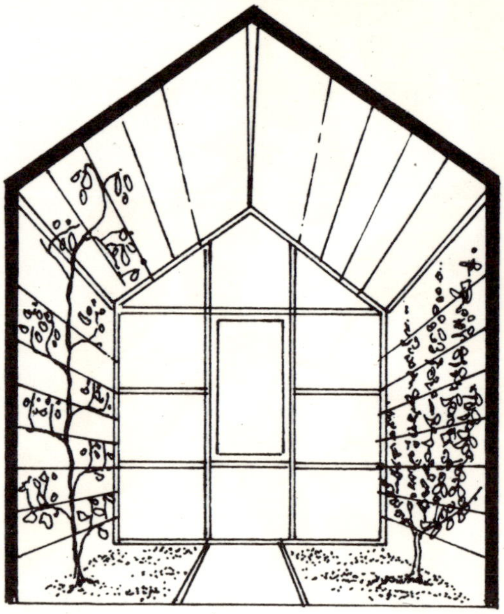

Training peaches

at the thought of allowing his precious plants to share the environment with anything other than himself.

The ideal then if you are to grow a specialist crop such as tomatoes or cucumbers is to provide an environment that will be as near the ideal as possible—there being no objection to washing down the greenhouse after clearing the finished crop, so that it can be followed with late flowering chrysanthemums. For the cost-conscious person this sort of rotation will be best as the greenhouse will produce more than enough to compensate for running costs. Although it may not be so interesting as the mixed bag of plants, the greenhouse that is used for specialist crops is much more efficient, as it can be thoroughly scrubbed down inside with mild disinfectant following the clearance of each crop—whatever is being grown one should bear in mind that hygiene is of paramount importance. When empty, if plants such as lettuce are grown in the soil, the ground can be dug over and prepare for the next crop by fertilizing, liming, sterilizing or whatever may be necessary. If the greenhouse is empty in winter during frosty weather it is wise to leave doors and vents open so that the frost can perform its own particular form of disease and pest control. Stretch a net across the door so that neighbourhood dogs and cats do not get in; it may be frosty inside, but will be colder still for them out.

Tomatoes

Tomatoes will be one of the most important and easiest crops for the greenhouse owner and can be simply raised from seed. New and, according to the seedsman, ever better varieties are continually becoming available, and it seems pointless to go into too much detail here when every packet of seed that you may purchase will be adequately provided with directions concerning sowing and growing. Purchase best quality seed from a reliable source is the best advice, and sow the seed as described elsewhere for seed sowing, bearing in mind that high temperatures in the region of 70°F (21°C) will be necessary for maximum germination. However, if only a small quantity of plants is required it is usually better to purchase them from a reliable nurseryman so that they can be planted out in March, being careful to select compact, sturdy plants rather than those that are tall and soft. Rotted manure should be dug into the soil as it is prepared, and the top dressed with a complete fertilizer with a dressing of lime where necessary at a rate of 4oz per sq. yd. (150g per sq. m). Before planting the soil must be at a temperature of not less than 55°F (13°C) and should be flooded with water, a check being made to ensure that the water has penetrated to a depth of about 18in (45cm).

Much will depend on the variety being grown, but when planting a space of about 18in (45cm) should be left between each plant. After planting, a stake should be put in alongside the plant, and string tied from the top of the stake to a wire strained across the top of the greenhouse on to which the plant can be trained. When growing, plants will need the maximum amount of light and air, provided it is not too cold, with the soil kept evenly moist—especially so once fruit has begun to form as erratic watering at that time will result in splitting of the fruits. An alternative to growing in the ground is that plants can be put in final pots of 10in (25cm) size, or large boxes, using good quality John Innes No. 3 growing mix. As plants grow care must be taken not to damage the flower trusses, and all growth that appears in the axil of the leaves should be removed, also any growth that may develop on the ends of fruiting trusses. Sun heat will be sufficient to keep plants in good fettle during the summer months, but it is advisable to maintain temperatures of not less than 60°F (15°C) at night to ensure active growth. Once plants have established and first fruits are forming it should be taken as a sign that regular

Tomatoes are a very economical crop to grow in the greenhouse

Left: Ring culture of tomatoes

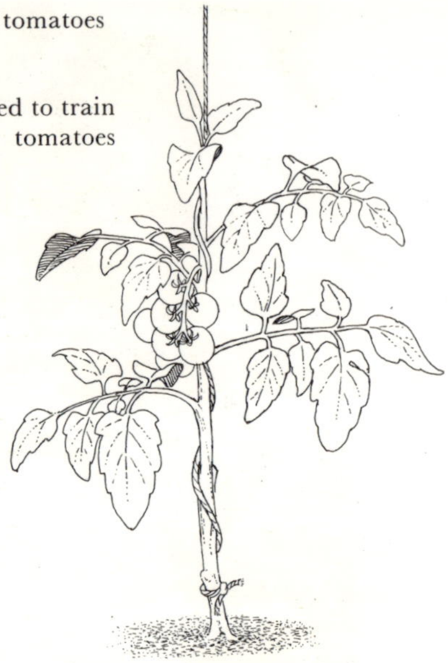

String being used to train tomatoes

Removing tomato sideshoots – keep doing this to encourage the plant to produce fruit not leaves

Training tomatoes

The peat bale culture method is one of the easiest ways of growing tomatoes

Tomatoes grow well in a greenhouse glazed to the ground

Cucumber 'Feminex' is a good variety

feeding must begin. There is no shortage of proprietary products for this purpose.

Cucumbers

Where the tomato requires a buoyant atmosphere in order to do well, the cucumber needs entirely the opposite in that the greenhouse must be warm and humid if they are to succeed. Consequently much higher temperatures will be needed, in the region of 65°F (18°C) as a minimum night temperature, and this may well discourage anyone who is sensitive concerning running costs. Seed should be sown early in the year, one to each small pot, and will germinate within the week in temperatures of around 70°F (21°C). Pots will rapidly fill with roots and plants should be moved into 5in (13cm) pots to establish further before they are planted out.

The best procedure is to plant cucumbers in ridged beds along the side of the house provided it is glazed to ground level. The area on which the bed is placed must be well drained and the bed itself composed of rich growing mix. As the roots penetrate the mix more can be added or a light mulch of strawy manure can be placed over the bed in order to feed the plants and retain moisture. Space plants about three feet apart and never plant too deeply. Growth is trained up wires strained along the house from one end to the other and about six inches away from the glass—the main stem should be tied in and allowed to go straight up without stopping until it has reached the ridge of the house. Fruit develops on side shoots growing from the main stem and should be tied to the lateral wires when long enough, the tie being made close to where the small fruits will be seen developing. Side growth should be stopped at one leaf joint beyond the developing fruit. Cucumbers have both male and female flowers, and it is important that the male flowers be removed as soon as they are seen to prevent cross fertilization, which would result in fruits developing seed and turning bitter—bees should be kept out of the greenhouse by covering the vents with close-meshed protective material as they are the principal offenders in respect of cross-fertilization. It is possible now to get all-female varieties. A light flick of shading will be beneficial and the interior of the house must always be kept moist by regularly using the hosepipe to damp down. Also, flicking the water over the undersides of the leaves will deter the troublesome red spider mites.

Melons

Although many gardeners think it contradictory, melons in the greenhouse, or outside for that

Tomato 'Sorrento Cross'

Three different ways to train cucumbers

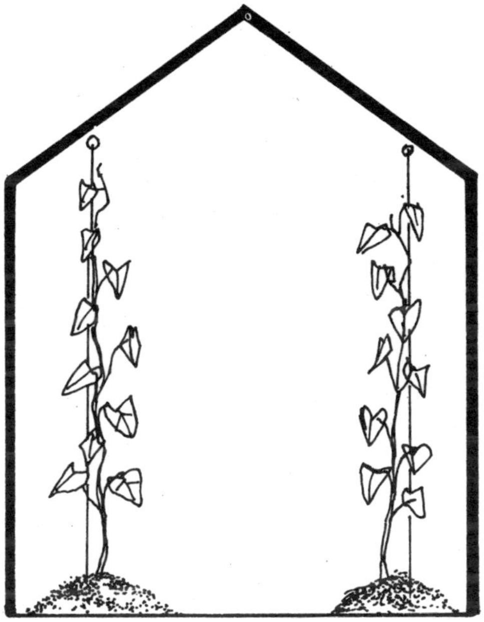

matter, are very much easier to care for than the cucumber. Plants are raised and trained in very much the same way as the cucumber, but the beds in which they are growing can be prepared on the greenhouse staging as each plant bears many fewer fruits—six to ten depending on the variety—which can be borne on a lesser amount of growth. Mulching and feeding is the same, but a net of some kind will have to be provided to support the fruit as it develops. In this instance, however, the female flowers must be fertilized by transferring pollen from the male flowers—the female flower is easily recognized by the fruit beginning to form in its centre. Plants recommended as having small fruits should be restricted to about ten melons, while larger fruiting plants must have no more than six. The growing tip is removed when the main stem is about three feet in length and lateral growth stopped at the second leaf. Should you have too many melons you can always fill the deep freeze with them.

Strawberries

Strawberries are less exotic than the melon, but a luxury nevertheless when one is able to have them out of season, which is possible in the small greenhouse where they can be housed with a wide variety of other plants. For this exercise young plants are rooted in small pots and gradually potted on as necessary until they are in 7in (18cm) pots, and plants are housed in a cold frame until

Melons make a satisfying greenhouse crop, visually and edibly

January when they can be taken into the greenhouse in relays of perhaps ten pots at a time.

Place them on a shelf near the glass and maintain temperatures in the region of 40–45°F (4–7°C). Feeding with weak liquid fertilizer should begin when flower buds appear, and the number of flowers should be reduced so that, depending on the vigour of the plant, none are bearing more than eight to twelve fruits. Fruits are very easily bruised and damaged, so each one should be held in place with a small cane to which the fruit is lightly tied. Treated in this way you can have the luxury experience of strawberries and cream a full month ahead of those in the garden.

Grapes

Due to ease of importing foreign produce hothouse grapes are no longer an economic proposition for the commercial grower, but there is no foreign produce that can compare with the luscious Black Hamburg grape when it is grown by an expert in specialized conditions. My memory takes me back to the days when greenhouses 30ft (9m) wide and 300ft (90m) in length were filled with lush foliage in the summer months providing shade for seemingly endless bunches of grapes that had taken more than a little skill to produce. Not the least skilful of the jobs was the one done by a team of women with long pointed scissors who deftly and quickly thinned out the bunches of grapes so that on marketing day symmetrical bunches of plump berries which were never overcrowded were offered for sale.

Although we are often advised to plant the root of the grape vine outside the greenhouse and to run the stem in through a hole in the wall for the growth to develop, this system was not practised in the commercial greenhouse. Here the vines were planted about three feet apart down either side of the house at the back, and the rods were supported on wires stretching from one end of the house to the other and about 15in (38cm) from the glass. It is best to use young plants when planting out and to ensure that the soil is rich, and to be very particular that it is well drained—this may mean digging a trench to provide a soakaway. During the first two years no fruit should be allowed to develop as these two years must be allowed for the plant to develop. Tie in the leading growth as it lengthens, but stop side growths when they are about 2ft (60cm) in length.

Due to severe pruning that is necessary the winter scene in the vine house is little more than bare rods and branches that have been scrubbed down to remove any mealy bug or other pests that had hoped to make their winter quarters beneath the loose bark. To discourage pests one can remove

Grapes need plenty of space, but are not difficult to grow

A healthy bunch of grapes

Rooting vine eyes

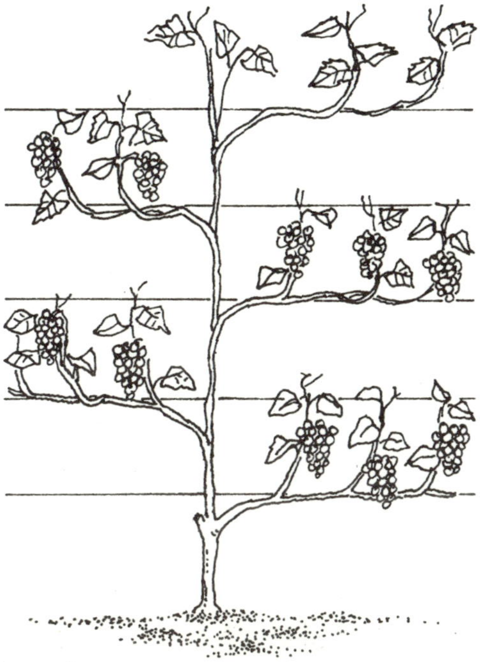

Training a vine

loose bark but care must be taken not to harm the green skin of the vine rod underneath. In November the previous season's growth is cut back to one or two eyes, and during the summer the tips of the new growth is pinched out regularly to prevent plants becoming too rampant. Several lengths of the firmer November's pruning can be retained for propagating new plants in February of the following year. These are simply done by cutting firm stems into sections about $1\frac{1}{2}$in (4cm) long, each piece to have an eye from which new growth will develop. With the eye uppermost the piece is pressed, not buried, into 3in (8cm) pots filled with sandy compost, which is subsequently kept in a propagator at about 65°F (18°C).

While actively growing plants will require a dung mulch over the roots, ample feeding and watering, and a very buoyant atmosphere in which to grow.

Vines may also be grown in large pots, 10in (25cm), using John Innes No. 3 that has been well firmed in the pot and adequately provided with drainage. Plants in pots should be provided with their own independent supports so that plants can be moved from one location to another as and when required. In the spring vigorous growth should be pruned back, care being taken not to damage flower clusters or fruit that one intends to harvest.

French Beans

Your arrival in the kitchen with a handful of appetizing French beans early in the month of May could well raise your value in the homestead.

Seedling sprouts off to a good start under glass

And it need not be too much of a problem if you can maintain temperatures in the region of 55°F (13°C) from January onwards when the beans are started. Half-fill a 10in (25cm) pot with John Innes No. 3 and sow ten seeds by pressing them gently into the growing mix, which must be kept fairly dry until the plants are growing away when water can be given more freely. The five weaker plants in the pot should be removed, and as the remaining five plants extend in length gradually more and more mix should be filled in around the stems until the pot is almost full. Regular fine spraying over of the foliage will deter pests and considerably benefit the plants, as will feeding with a liquid fertilizer once they are established in their pots.

Other vegetables

Besides these more exotic fruits one can manage a very wide range of more ordinary vegetables in the greenhouse and this was brought home to me only recently on visiting a commercial grower who had given over one of his greenhouses to an aging father so that he could have his 'allotment' in the dry. In the dry, indeed—the old boy's crop of cabbages, potatoes, carrots, turnips and what have you looked far more profitable than the houses filled with tomatoes that at the time were not in great demand. So the advice if you are tempted to grow vegetables in the greenhouse is to go ahead, not to be afraid to experiment and to grow them in pots or borders, whichever is the more convenient. Bear in mind, however, that Brussels sprouts in a 7in (18cm) pot could just be a tiny bit ridiculous! It is also wise to remember with plants that must be cut as they mature, lettuce for example, that it is important to grow them in very small batches so avoiding the embarrassment of having fifty ready one weekend and none the next!

Lettuce 'Giant Perfection'

9
Orchids

My first sight of the interior of a greenhouse filled with cymbidiums during their resting period could well be described as my most disappointing horticultural experience. Orchids, in spite of their high rating of being possibly the most exotic of all flowers, often leave much to be desired when one sees the plants from which they emerge. Nevertheless, there is no doubting that the presence of orchids in flower will add a new dimension to almost any greenhouse. And, though many of them are best left to the specialist, a surprising number will be found reasonably easy to manage when sharing the greenhouse with an assortment of other subjects. The principal requirements, in common with a wide range of greenhouse plants, are warmth, moisture, light and a suitable potting medium.

Many would-be orchid growers are put off by the whispered comment that it takes seven (magical number) years to grow a plant from seed. But it also takes seven years to grow a tulip or daffodil from seed—and when did you last purchase a packet of tulip seed? You begin by buying bulbs, and with orchids you make a start by purchasing young plants, or older ones if you can afford them! When purchasing, the thing to do is to shop around as there is considerable variation in price between the different suppliers, and to inform the chosen supplier of the greenhouse conditions you can provide, so that plants suited to these conditions are acquired. And it goes without saying that the beginner should not be too ambitious with earlier ventures into the growing of orchids which can get quite a hold on you if some of my drooling colleagues are anything to go by!

My good friend Bill Swanson is almost the perfect example of a man with a medium size greenhouse who, as a matter of interest, picked up three or four orchids from an exhibitor at the close of a flower show. These were given first the most favoured spot in the greenhouse—in a corner where they could almost be paid homage to every morning as one would a shrine. The collection gradually built up until part of the greenhouse was sectioned off to accommodate the ever increasing numbers, which were mostly plants requiring lower temperatures. In time the plants were transferred to a new house with a deep frame outside where plants could spend the summer months. He frequently mentioned prices paid for some of his new pets and a lump came into my throat to match the price to the often tatty bit of plant that was the result of the transaction! Had there been an instant display of exotic blooms to compensate for the outlay one could have understood, but there was more often than not several years delay before the first feeble flower crept into view. My friend Bill would pick it up and view this wonder of nature in the same way as a devoted guide dog does his master, but enthusiastic comments from this canny Scottish body were seldom forthcoming. The cost of purchasing the plant initially and the growing on time amounted, in my eyes, to little more than an economic nightmare.

From the foregoing it is hoped that the reader has got the message that, before venturing into the exotic world of cattleyas, miltonias, paphiopedilums (cypripediums) and the like, it would be wise to visit the greenhouse of the local enthusiast and to tot up the cost of establishing a collection and maintaining it. In such a greenhouse you will see the sort of display and collection you can expect—whereas by visiting the professional you will see plants growing at their best in conditions vastly different to those one could normally expect to maintain in your own greenhouse.

Temperature and ventilation

To make a reasonably satisfactory job of growing orchids it would be necessary to have, say, three greenhouses so that cool, intermediate and warm temperatures could be provided. Also, with different houses it would be possible to shade the house to the degree required by particular plants. But three greenhouses would be a luxury in respect of cost and space and worry (an important side) quite beyond the scope of most of us, so it is wise to choose plants that are reasonably compatible and to maintain conditions accordingly. Cymbidium plants, for example, would require several feet of head room, whereas odontoglossums would be more in keeping with less spacious surroundings.

Adequate circulation of air is a further major consideration, and this will mean fitting the greenhouse with slatted staging rather than the more conventional gravel covered base to stand plants on. In spite of the need for air it is also important that there should be a humid feeling around the plants. This will mean putting a thick layer of moisture-retaining gravel or coke breeze under the staging which should be damped down as an almost automatic reaction as one waters the plants on the staging. The pathway will also have to be regularly damped—the resultant rising moisture helping the plants considerably.

Temperature should be regulated to give as near the ideal as possible for all the various plants that one will be likely to have, bearing in mind that cool-loving plants growing in warm conditions will suffer just as much as the more tender ones will in cooler temperatures. It is important when acquiring plants to ensure that they are suited to the conditions that are likely to prevail—although it would be impossible to list all the possible permutations here, there is a guidance list at the end of this chapter suggesting plants for cool, intermediate and warmer conditions.

Growing mediums

There is always an air of mystery concerning the potting medium used by the man who is successful with the growing of his plants, and a reluctance on his part to divulge the information. And in probably no other field of horticulture is there greater secrecy concerning growing mixes than in that of orchid growing. The simple answer would be to suggest that when purchasing plants one should at the same time ask the supplier to sell a quantity of his own growing medium. Many of them do and this will save the considerable bother involved in accumulating the diverse ingredients that you are likely to be recommended to use. But we must not shirk the duty by opting out in this way, as it may just be possible that you have such mysterious ingredients as osmunda fibre (it looks like the matted stuffing from a horse hair sofa!), fir tree bark and sphagnum moss lying about in the potting shed just waiting to be used! Whatever else, the potting medium must be open and fibrous, allowing ample passage of air around the roots—this is particularly important in respect of the epyphytic types that make their natural home amongst the trees. A suggested mix for these is two parts osmunda fibre to one part fresh sphagnum moss with a dusting of charcoal to keep the mixture sweet, but it is fully appreciated that the orchid man will soon develop Bill Swanson's trait of devising new and ever more exciting mixtures almost every week! For terrestial plants the mix need not be so open and the following is suggested: equal parts peat, fibrous loam, fresh sphagnum moss and sand.

Sharp draining of the growing mix is essential, so it is important not just to 'crock' the pot in the conventional sense, but to place a good layer of crocks in the bottom of the pot before introducing the potting mix. As plants are potted on into larger pots, so the layer of crocks in the bottom of the pot should be increased in depth.

Many of the plants with more pendulous flowers look better and grow better when planted up in open, wood-slatted baskets which are lined with moss before introducing the compost and the plant. Plants growing in this way will require very frequent watering other than at their normal resting time when much less water is needed.

Cattleya Propagated by division (or from seed if the demanding facilities are available) there are a number of species and a vast number of hybrids in a wealth of different colours. Good light with some shade from strong sunlight is needed, and lots of humidity. Potting is necessary after flowering every second or third year, or clump can be divided up into sections of not less than four pseudobulbs that are potted up individually. Care must be taken to avoid overwatering after potting up, but plants will benefit from having foliage sprayed over regularly.

Cymbidium One of the most spectacular of all the orchids, often with several flower spikes bearing many flowers on one plant. However,

Orchid 'Vanda sanderiana'

although they are among the easiest to care for, they will require ample space in which to grow, and will need a temperature in the region of 50°F (10°C) and shaded glass during the summer.

Pot on every other year after flowering using slightly heavier compost. Plants flower during the first six months of the year, and resent disturbance, so resist the temptation to separate them. Ample watering and feeding with weak liquid fertilizer will be needed while plants are actively growing, while much less water is needed in winter, although the growing mix should not become excessively dry.

Dendrobium Needing a minimum temperature in the region of 50°F (10°C) this is another genus with many species and hybrids which flowers during the winter months. Not very demanding, they are well within the scope of the greenhouse owner able to maintain the suggested minimum temperature, and you could have an interesting and colourful collection by filling the house with a selection of the many different dendrobiums.

Epidendrum Reasonably easy to grow in good light, many will flower almost throughout the year, and *E. fragrans* will further enhance the scene by producing flowers with a delicate aroma. Free growing, they are excellent plants for hanging from the roof of the house, or *E. radicans* may be encouraged to climb for several feet if given a moist support to cling to.

Miltonia These are most attractive plants with short upright stems bearing flowers that resemble large and exotic pansies of uncommonly brilliant colouring. Plants are small and need little space, but must have adequate moisture during their growing period. Light shade is needed in summer and good light in winter with intermediate temperature.

Paphiopedilum There are many species of the slipper orchid and almost countless hybrids and, by careful selection, you could have plants in flower almost throughout the year. Moisture with lots of humidity is essential, feeding with weak fertilizer during the summer months and shade from strong sunlight are necessary. Being terrestial, plants require slightly heavier growing mix when potting on, and to increase plants they should be divided in spring.

A few plants for 40–50, 50–60, 60–70°F (4–10, 10–15, 15–21°C) temperature ranges follow. An orchid catalogue should be consulted by the greenhouse owner determined to specialize in orchids.

Cool 40–50°F (4–10°C)

Coelogyne cristata, 2–3in (5–8cm) high, 6in (15cm) spikes up to seven pure white fragrant flowers on each, with centre of lip pale orange. Flowers December to March.
Cymbidium dayanum, 12in (30cm) high, pendulous flower stems, carrying several scented flowers 3in (8cm) across. Flowers have white petals with purple centre streak, and a white lip with purple and yellow markings. Flowers in October.
Cypripedium reginae, 1½–3ft (45–90cm) tall, four 4in (10cm) wide flowers on each stem, pure white, with lip heavily mottled with rose-purple. Flowers June and July.
Dendrobium kingianum, 2–4in (5–10cm) high, with two to six flowers, 1in (2·5cm) across, yellow tinged with red or purple, deep violet lip with white margins. Flowers April and May.
Maxillaria picta, 2–3in (5–8cm) high, flower stems 4in (10cm) high, carrying flowers 2in (5cm) wide, yellow with red and purple marks, December to February.

Intermediate 50–60°F (10–15°C)

Calanthe masuca, evergreen, with erect arching flower stems 2–3ft (60–90cm) long. Violet-purple flowers from June to October.
Cattleya bowringiana, 24in (60cm) high, 8in (20cm) flower stems with five to ten flowers on each, 4in (10cm) across, light rose-purple, dark purple edges on lips, flowers September to December.
Cattleya skinneri, 9in (23cm) high, 3in (8cm) flower stems, five to nine flowers 3in (8cm) across, pale pink/purple, with white lip, March to June.
Coelogyne massangeana, 3–4in (8–10cm) high, flower stems to 24in (60cm), up to 30 flowers per plant, 2in (5cm) across, yellow-brown, sepia lip with white veins, January to August.
Cymbidium eburneum, 8–12in (20–30cm) flower stems, three flowers on each, 4in (10cm) across, ivory white with yellow band down centre of white lip, April and May.
Dendrobium nobile, 18in (45cm) high, flowers 2–3in (5–8cm) across, two or three to each stem, white at base, mauve at tips, dark maroon lip edged with yellow, January to March.
Epidendrum fragrans, 3–4in (8–10cm) high, 9in (23cm) flower stem with two to five flowers, 3in (8cm) across on each, cream or yellow, white lip with purple stripe, scented, August to October.
Maxillaria nasuta, 3in (8cm) high, single star like flowers 1–1½in (2·5–3cm) across on 4in (10cm)

Nepenthes orchid growing on bark

stems, pale yellow/green, suffused maroon on back, March to September.

Warm 60–70°F (15–21°C)

Cattleya dowiana, 12in (30cm) high, 5in (13cm) flower stems, flowers 6–8in (15–20cm) across, golden yellow with red veined lip, five to six blooms on each stem, October to December.
Dendrobium aureum, 12in (30cm) high, two or three flowers on each stem, cream white or yellow with golden lip, streaked with red, fragrant, January and February.
Dendrobium moschatum, up to 5ft (150cm) high, seven to fifteen flowers up to 3in (8cm) across, pale yellow with purple veins, pale yellow lip with maroon patches, scented, May to July.
Epidendrum nocturnum, to 3ft (90cm) high, 12–24in (30–60cm) flower stem, single fragrant 4in (10cm) wide flower, yellow green with white lip, March to May.
Phalaenopsis lueddemainniana, 6in (15cm) stem, 24in (60cm) flower spike, 2in (5cm) wide flowers, white with amethyst stripes, lip white with purple lobe, May and June.
Vanda caerulea, stems around 4ft (120cm), fifteen flowers on each, $3\frac{1}{2}$–4in (9–10cm) across, pale blue, purple, lip, blue-white side lobes, August to November.

A tubular heater will provide even heat for a warm orchid house (courtesy of Humex)

10 Cacti and Succulents

I often wonder where an interest in any particular plant may have its beginnings—with cacti it could well go back to ones school days, as it is an established fact among producers of these plants for retail sale that there is a marked increase in sales when the kids are on holiday. However one might have begun there is little doubt about the firm division of opinion concerning cacti—you either like them or you don't.

Heat and light

Although the majority come from desert regions of the world this should not imply that they require excessive heat and very arid conditions at all times. It is difficult to generalize with such a vast range of plants, but as a general rule, you could develop an interesting collection of cacti and succulents yet not have the greenhouse heated to more than 45°F (7°C) during the winter months. During this period of the year plants are resting and, although they may seem to shrivel a little and look the worse for wear they will be far better in this condition than if they were watered and made to look plumper and more healthy.

The true enthusiast would in all probability frown at the thought of having plants of any other sort than cacti and succulents in his greenhouse, but my own small collection never seem to object to sharing with all manner of oddments from the wonderful world of plants. Possibly not the most grand specimens of their kind in the world, but they do pretty well on their shelf along the back of the greenhouse—however, one must agree that the specialist house filled with the same type of plant always has the edge on similar plants forming part of the mixed collection house.

In any event cacti will need maximum light to do well, and in the summer there should also be plenty of air circulating around them. During the warmer months of the year the less precious plants in the collection can be placed out of doors in a sheltered, sunny position—even the precious ones would come to no harm if they occupied a well-ventilated cold frame in summer if greenhouse space is limited. (My problem when putting plants out for the summer in this way is that other things by some strange means seem to fill the indoor area, with the consequence that there is little room for anything when the day of reckoning comes and they are all in need of the precious bench space again!)

Propagation

The layman is frequently much impressed by the cactus grower who can show his plants off with beautiful flowers surmounting their more than spiteful spines—it could well be thought that the man with the plants has something of the midas touch about him. But it is not so very difficult to have quite a good selection of cacti in flower in the early summer months, and they need not be the most expensive and ancient of plants. You can grow from seed in three years if you have a mind to—this will mean acquiring seed, named for preference, and sowing in J.I. seed mixture to which a liberal amount of sharp sand is added. If the seed is fresh the germination percentage may surprise you, and it really only needs conventional treatment by sowing in seed boxes and covering the box with a sheet of glass, and maintaining temperatures in the region of 65°F (18°C). There should be no great hurry to take seedlings from the box, as they will do well enough to grow on there for a while. Eventually, from the seed box they are transferred to similar boxes and given an inch or so of room all round.

Cacti are generally increased from cuttings *Left:* taking a cutting from a mature plant *Above:* making a hole with a pointed stick *Bottom left:* inserting the cutting and firming down *Bottom right:* finished and labelled

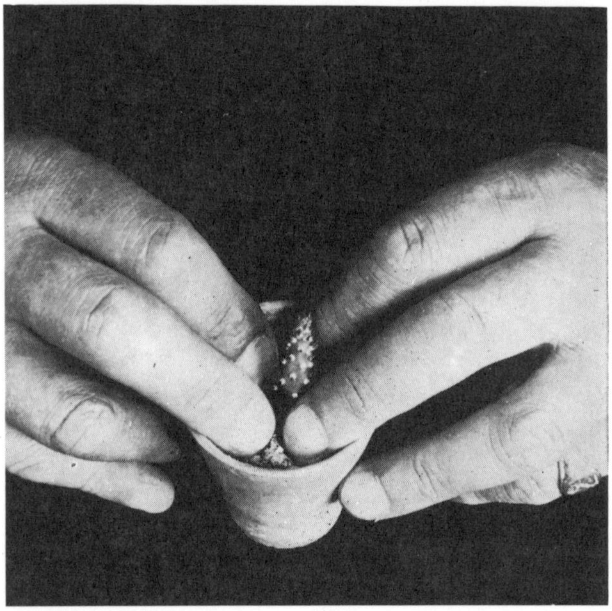

A suitable growing mix for this move would be the following: J.I. No. 2 mix to which additional coarse sand or grit has been added, plus a small quantity of old mortar rubble or crushed brick. Almost the most important requirement for growing mix for potting cacti is that it should be very free draining. In boxes with reasonable growing mix, or seed pans for small quantities, young plants will establish more rapidly than in pots and can be left until plants are touching before being potted into small pots. Small, square pots are useful at this stage as pots can set out tightly grouped so that there is no staging visible, which will prevent weeds growing there. At all costs when potting the temptation to put plants into pots that are excessively large should be avoided—potting on should be done in very easy stages.

Going back to growing mix, it is almost inevitable that you will develop your own in time, as almost every grower of plants whatever they may be will devise his own special mixture that is considered to be far superior to anything else that could possibly be suggested. And there will be differing mixtures for the different cacti and succulents that are being grown—Christmas and Easter cactus (schlumbergeras, for example) would require more peat and less sand than is suggested here. When potting cacti there is always the problem of getting the more spiteful ones from one pot to the other without drawing blood. One way of overcoming the difficulty is to use salad serving tongs to hold the plant as it is potted with the free hand. Another is to use rolled paper to make a collar around the plant—the ends of the paper being held with one hand while the potting is done with the other. My own method is to use an empty pot of the same size and shape as the one the plant is being transferred from and to pot the empty pot into the new mixture. When the pot is removed, if the growing mix is reasonably moist, a perfect mould will be there to drop the plant into when it has been removed from its pot.

Soil borne diseases cause damage to the root system of the plant which in turn is seen when the apparently healthy plant topples over leaving little more than a mushy, rotting mess. Strict hygiene in all aspects of plant handling is one way of counteracting disease, as is the need for sharply drained mix that never remains saturated. When root diseases are suspected it is wise to take the precaution of watering benomyl solution into the growing mix. Likewise red spider mite may be controlled by watering a proprietary systemic insecticide into the soil. Another of the most troublesome of pests is mealy bug, which finds its way into the most inaccessible parts of your plants. Mild attacks may be treated in the traditional manner by dabbing the affected areas with a small brush that has been soaked in methylated spirits, or in severe cases the plants may be sprayed with malathion solution, care being taken not to treat plants too indiscriminately, however, as some of the crassulas are susceptible to malathion. Scale insects may also be controlled with malathion, although it may be necessary to use a sponge soaked in the insecticide to wipe the scales from the plants.

There follows a very small selection of the many plants that one may acquire with little trouble, either by sowing seed, or by purchasing them from a recognized producer.

Astrophytum myriostigma the bishop's cap cactus gets its very apt common name from the five evenly shaped ribs that are smooth and free from spines. Flowers are yellow and appear during the summer. Not difficult plants to manage if they have a dry resting period in winter and well aired, sunny house during the summer months.

Cephalocereus senilis is an attractive slow growing plant of cylindrical shape which is completely covered in grey hairs, giving the plant the highly applicable common name of old man cactus. Not in the least difficult to care for provided you are always sparing with water. If greenhouse space is limited plants may remain in the same spot for many years in order to restrain their growth and no harm will be done.

Cereus peruvianus is one of the more typical cactus plants and grows reasonably fast, so will require potting on as the plant becomes disproportionate in relation to the container in which it is growing.

Chamaecereus silvestrii grows to only a few inches in height, is silver in colour, and produces clusters of growth with a silvery, fishnet pattern. Plants will tolerate slight frost in the greenhouse provided the compost is bone dry—dry and cold in winter could well result in bright red flowers in summer. Individual pieces can be broken off and rooted at any time, making this one of the easiest of all plants to propagate. Best grown in shallow pans.

Echinocactus grusonii is possibly the finest of all the lower growing cacti and is commonly named the golden barrel cactus because of its rounded shape and rich yellow colouring. Given conventional treatment they are not difficult to care for, but growth is painfully slow and plants take many years to mature. The yellow spines of the plant are particularly attractive, but it is wise not to get too close to them!

Epiphyllum Known as the orchid cactus, these have the most wonderful flowers in late summer, flowers that are so striking in colour they can truly be described as breath taking. The trumpet shaped flowers are stalkless and produced directly from the edges of the leaves, and last for but a few days, but there will be quite a succession from the fat flower buds that are a continual source of excitement as one waits for the next wonder of nature to unfold. New plants can be easily propagated from pieces of the plants cut up into sections about 4in (10cm) long and put in a propagator. Eipiphyllums need an acid growing mix that is rich in humus, in the way of peat, leafmould and a little sphagnum moss worked in to keep the mix open. Plants also require lightly shaded conditions and temperatures in the region of 60°F (15°C). They are also more succulent than cactus in appearance and will happily mix with other plants in the greenhouse.

Lobivia Another example of the barrel type cactus with deep ribs and prominent spines, which produces flowers from around the sides of the plant. Plants are small and compact and must have a dry resting period in winter to induce them to flower in early summer. An interesting feature of the name is that it is an anagram of Bolivia—the country from which the plant originates.

Mammillaria Needing little space, these are fine plants that could well provide an interesting side to any collection of plants as there are so many of them. Flowers are small but are produced with little difficulty, and it is wise to save seed where possible so that there are young plants coming on to replace older ones which are susceptible to root rot Mammillarias can be particularly attractive when crowded growth is seen well-filling shallow pans.

Opuntia These develop into plants of considerable size, even in the small greenhouse and will, almost inevitably, provide a home for countless mealy bugs. Although there are varieties with more cylindrical shape, the best known opuntias are those with large spine covered pads of growth which protrude in all directions as the plant ages. No special treatment is required, and new plants can be raised by removing individual pads and cutting an inch or so off the bottom and allowing them to dry before inserting in sandy growing mix.

Schlumbergera Probably better known as zygocactus, and surely by the common name of Christmas cactus—although it does not always oblige by flowering at that particular time, or flowering at all for that matter! Flowers in attractive shades of pink are produced from the ends of pad-like stems of growth, and may drop off without apparent reason, but this is frequently due to the location of the plants being changed as it comes into flower or through radical changes in the amount of water given. Temperature variations may also cause flowers and buds to drop. Easily propagated from pieces of stem that break off easily where one pad joins the other. Grow on in J.I. No. 1 potting mix.

Succulents

Although some of these, such as agaves and aloes, would in time become too large for the garden greenhouse, there is a very wide range of succulents that will add interest to any collection. Many, such as the kalanchoes, flower quite freely, but the majority are grown for their interesting and attractive foliage. Echeverias are especially interesting, with their blue metallic colouring and a 'bloom' that is also attractive, but which can be ruined by careless handling. For the most incapable of propagators there should be no problem when attempting to raise new plants of *Kalanchoe tubiflora* and *K. daigremontiana*, as they both produce perfectly proportioned miniature plants along the edges of their leaves—if left to their own ends these may be left until they fall off naturally where they will grow in the greenhouse staging. They will grow anywhere, really, so it is wise to discipline oneself to having only one or two plants for interest's sake as they are not particularly attractive as mature plants. Almost all the succulents will do well in the light, airy house in conditions that err on the dry side—wet, badly lighted conditions are especially harmful to them.

11 Bulbs

Almost all the spring flowering bulbs that are seen in the garden can be had in flower in the greenhouse much earlier in the year. Before planting it is wise to select the container that suits the particular bulb, so that crocus and *Iris reticulata*, for example, are grown either in small pots or shallow pans with the result that growth and container are in proportion. Pots must be well drained, so a layer of crocks in the bottom of the pot before putting in the growing mix should be considered essential. A good general mix is J.I. No. 1. Bulbs can also be induced to flower for Christmas, but these must be pre-cooled and should be specially asked for from your supplier.

Potting up

Bulbs can be potted up in October, and if daffodils are planted in larger pots a double layer of bulbs can be put in to give a very fine display; this is

Crocuses in pots can give an early flowering start to the greenhouse year

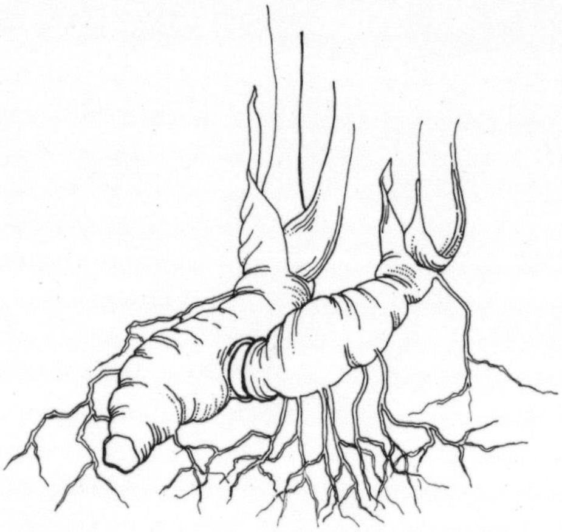

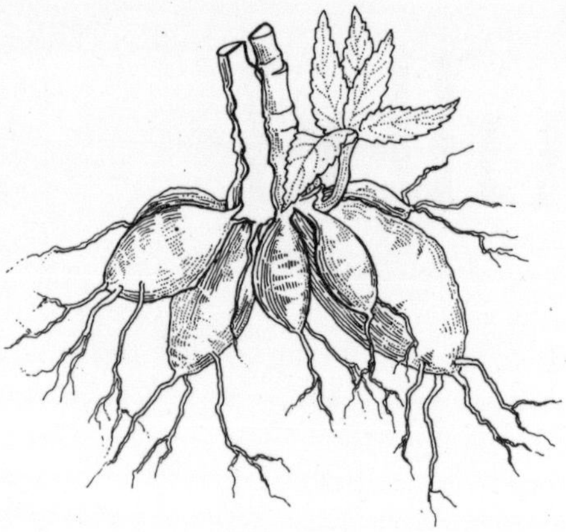

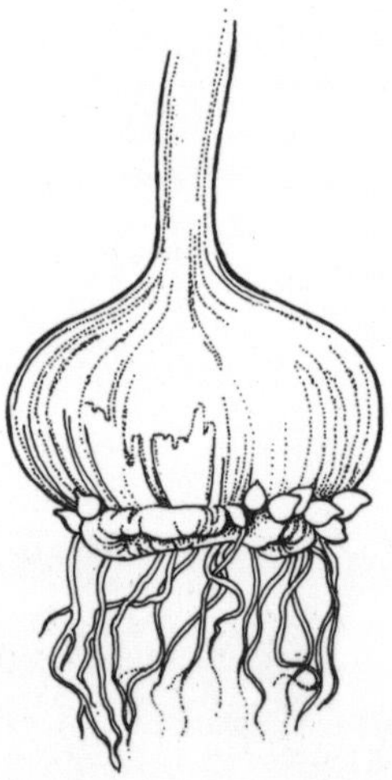

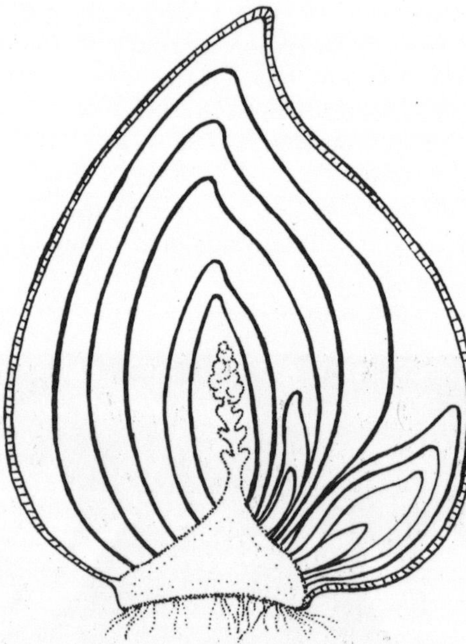

A rhizome, a tuber, a corm and a bulb

This diagram shows the root development of bulbs

done by half filling the pot with growing mix and planting a layer of bulbs, then filling the remaining area and putting in a further lot. Bulbs can be placed quite close together with the tops of the upper layer just showing through the mix. After planting, bulbs are left out of doors for the root system to develop. It is best to clear an area against a sheltered wall, and to cover the ground with sand on to which the plant pots are placed. The pots are then completely covered with sand, with at least a 3in (8cm) layer on top of the pots. The soil should never dry out, but you must avoid the possibility of having the mix saturated for long periods. When growth can be seen pushing through the sand it will be time to move the pots to slightly warmer conditions, possibly to a cold frame first so that they can be gradually accustomed to warmer temperatures. It is wise to provide three or four stakes around the pot with looped string to support taller growing bulbs, so that they are neat and more manageable when taken indoors which will probably be the case for many of them.

There may be the temptation to plant up a selection of mixed bulbs in the same containers, and there is no reason why they should not all do perfectly well, but it is infinitely more attractive to see bulbs of the same variety and colour growing in the same pot.

Greenhouse bulbs

Besides the hardy outdoor bulbs there is also a wide range of tender kinds that the greenhouse owner will find it possible to grow. Some such as *Hymenocallis ovata* from tropical South America will require temperatures in the region of 60°F

Lilium lankongense

(15°C) if they are to survive but not all are so demanding.

Hippeastrums are one of the best known of the tender bulbs, and these are not difficult to manage in reasonable warmth. Treated bulbs may be bought that will flower at Christmas and will have full directions supplied concerning their treatment, but whatever else it will be important to maintain temperatures in the region of 70°F (21°C) if they are in fact going to flower for the festive season. Many of these bulbs are now actually sold in their growing pots with appropriate compost and only need be watered for them to get under way. In modest conditions indoors or in the greenhouse they will not be difficult to bring into flower, but there is often some confusion about how they should be treated after they have flowered. Frequently there is a tendency to neglect the plant with the thought that it has done its work. But, given proper treatment hippeastrums will outlast the owner, and proper treatment will mean feeding the growing mix regularly after the plants has flowered until such time as the leaves begin to yellow naturally and die. As leaves yellow the amount of water is gradually reduced until such time as the soil is quite dry, when the bulbs can be placed under the greenhouse staging on their sides so that no water can get into the pot. There may be nothing in it but many of the older school advocate that the bulbs should be warmed on the hot pipes in the greenhouse or over a radiator indoors in February prior to planting so that there is added assurance that the bulb will produce its flower. Following the first seasons growth it is wise to pot the bulb in February into a 6in (15cm) pot using J.I. No. 2 growing mix. Thereafter it can be left in the same pot for several years, with perhaps a top dressing of fresh mix when the bulb is started into growth—prior to top dressing some of the old mix should be removed from around the top of the pot.

Nerines In recent years a cut flower that is seen more and more in the better class flower shop is the nerine, with bell-shaped flowers mainly in shades of pink on stems some 18in (45cm) long. Nerines can be grown out of doors if planted in the border at the foot of a south-facing wall. Plants may be raised from seed, but it is a very long and slow business, so it is much better to acquire bulbs and to increase them by planting the small bulbs that grow around the parent. Bulbs are comparatively small and should be planted to half their depth in rich compost in late summer. Nerines are indigenous to South Africa and produce new growth

Nerines are an easy but very attractive glasshouse bulb

A narrow-leaved croton plant

Lapageria rosea, a member of the lily family, makes a most attractive plant

Right: Lilium superbum

between September and May and should be kept bone dry and rested between May and September. Little space is needed for them, they can have their pots crowded together and be placed on a shelf near the glass where they can enjoy full sunlight. Frequent potting is not necessary, but bulbs will need feeding when they are in active growth. Flowers appear before the leaves and you should start watering in late summer as soon as flowers appear, and in mid-September even if there are no flowers evident. Temperature is not important provided the house is light and airy, but bulbs in pots should not be exposed to frost.

Cape Cowslip Another colourful South African bulb is the Cape Cowslip, *lachenalia*, of which there are many fine colours, some varieties having spotted leaves to add to the attraction. Pot bulbs almost touching in 5in (13cm) pots in August using J.I. No. 2 mix, with the bulbs only just covered. Alternatively the bulbs can be planted in a hanging basket to provide aerial subjects with a difference. Water after potting and place the bulbs in a cold frame until November—from there they are transferred to the greenhouse where the temperature should remain in the region of 50°F (10°C). A shelf where they will get plenty of light and air will suit them. As more foliage is produced, so more water will be required, and feed should be given as plants are coming into flower. Following flowering, gradually give less water until the growing mix is quite dry—during the summer bulbs will benefit from being baked in the sun until it is time to shake them out and pot into fresh mix in August, so that the cycle can begin all over again. Plants can be increased by means of offsets planted up individually, or from seed sown in a warm propagator. Plants grow between September and June and rest for the remainder of the year.

Hymenocallis Mention was made earlier of the tropical bulbous plant, *Hymenocallis*, which requires very much warmer conditions than any of those already discussed. Plants require rich growing mix and annual potting until they are in 10in (25cm) pots where they can remain for several years provided feeding is not neglected

Lilies make a splendid greenhouse crop – this is *Lilium* 'Bellingham'

during the summer months. Mature plants have broad green leaves that are about 2ft (60cm) long, and the flowers when they appear in late summer have stalks of similar length. A number of white spidery flowers are produced on each stem, and the life overall would be about ten days. Not a long time it may be felt for a plant needing minimum temperature of 60°F (15°C) and one which is fairly space demanding into the bargain. But one has only to enter the greenhouse with one of these plants in flower and there is an almost immediate twitching of the nostrils in an effort to detect the source of the heady fragrance that pervades the atmosphere. Perhaps it is unfair to mention a personal favourite in the plant world when there is the sure knowledge that any would-be purchaser would find a source of supply almost impossible to locate—still, one may also feel that there are still one or two things in the plant world that remain rather precious!

12 Pests and Diseases

In the agreeable confines of a heated greenhouse pests, if they go unchecked, will multiply at an alarming rate. So, whatever chemical may be recommended as a suitable cure, it should be borne in mind by the greenhouse owner that the practice of prevention of pests is much more satisfactory, and a great deal cheaper. But it should be remembered that prevention may be expensive in respect of one's time, as it will entail a great deal more work by way of maintaining conditions that underline the meaning of hygiene. Dead leaves and rotting material of every descrip-

Vine weevils

tion should be strictly for the dustbin, and this will entail at least a twice weekly check over and tidy up.

Often someone with experience of greenhouse management, the good grower if you like, develops an almost instinctive nose for trouble and can detect the signs of red spider being present long before the plant shows indications of physical damage. But there is no chance of the inexperienced grower learning these inborn skills through reading these pages—the one who can detect trouble in its infancy is similar to the green-fingered gardener, and there is no book that will teach you how to acquire greenfingers!

Checking for pests

One of the best ways of checking for pests is to physically pick up plants and inspect them before setting them over on staging gravel that has been freshly raked to receive them. A waste of time you may think, but it is amazing how much better

Damping off

almost every plant will look in a fresh location, and it is even more amazing the things you will see on a plant when you pick it up compared to how little you see on passing it by every day.

Aphids are among the most common of pests both in the greenhouse and the garden, and you will usually find these clustering around the soft young growth at the tip of the plant. Not a very troublesome pest if you see them in time.

Whitefly normally congregate on the undersides of leaves and can present a massive problem if they are allowed to get out of hand. These are easily detected by inspecting the undersides of leaves, or simply by tapping the plant and seeing the triangular shaped flies dart about in all directions. Here, persistence is an essential quality in attempting to control these very determined pests and that will mean spraying the undersides of leaves with recommended insecticides at frequent intervals—every ten days so that you catch the young ones as they hatch out and are less resistant to the chemical. For some plants they appear to have a particular fondness, among them cinerarias, fuchsias and poinsettias.

Galls on azalea

Almost everyone with a greenhouse will recognise mealy bug, which looks like a small white woodlouse and rolls its young up in protective balls of what would appear to be a good substitute for cotton wool. You can control the odd few bugs by dabbing them with cotton wool that has been soaked in appropriate insecticide or methylated spirits, but this advice would have little more than joke value for the man who has a rampant grape vine, stephanotis or hoya plant entangling its way around the top of the greenhouse. The best advice for him would, of course, be not to have such invasive plants in a small greenhouse when they are known to harbour all the pests in christendom. But if you have the thing above your head with its appropriate quota of beasties, then you can only thoroughly, thoroughly, thoroughly saturate the tangled growth with malathion liquid insecticide at very frequent intervals and hope to have some measure of control. Root mealy bug is not such a problem and can be checked by drenching the compost thoroughly with malathion solution. Or, if preferred, the soil and beasties can be washed off the roots and the plant re-potted in fresh mix.

Rust on antirrhinum

Red spider mite is possibly the most troublesome of all the pests in the greenhouse, as they are almost impossible to detect with the naked eye, are difficult to eradicate, and are very harmful to a vast number of plants, both edible and decorative. Tiny pin prick holes on the undersides of leaves are usually the first indication of their presence, which is followed by finely traced webs across the back of the leaf veins and between petiole and leaf margin around the petiole. In hot, dry conditions mites will increase rapidly, and their continual sucking action will result in plants taking on a harder, brownish look. In severe attacks the leaves will curl down and inwards from their edges and in time 'ropes' of red spider webs will hang from the plant. Hopefully, by then you will have given up

Ray blight on chrysanthemum

Botrytis on carnation

greenhouse gardening and sought some other form of recreation!

Scale insects in some instances appear to be a natural brown marking on the plant, as they seem quite immobile and are very uniform in shape—the young ones are flesh coloured and the older scales a light brown. When older scales die their husks provide a natural shelter under which young can take refuge. A mild attack may be controlled by wiping the scales off the plant with a sponge that have been soaked in malathion solution. More widespread attacks may be controlled by thoroughly spraying the plant with malathion, or white oil emulsion. Used at three monthly intervals the latter may be used as an effective deterrent against many pests and at the same time will impart attractive gloss to the leaves of plants with a natural shine to their leaves, philodendrons and ficus being good examples.

As it makes its intricate patterns through the leaves of such plants as chrysanthemums the leaf miner is probably the easiest of all pests to detect and can be killed simply by detecting the pest inside the leaf and squashing it—BHC or malathion can be used to control more widespread attacks.

Eelworm can be a crippling problem for many plants as the worms actually move about in the roots and within the plant itself, and it is extremely difficult for the small greenhouse owner to control. Plants that may be attacked are lettuce, tomatoes, cucumbers, many of the bulbous plants, chrysanthemums and hydrangeas, and an indication of the presence is swollen and malformed growth, and a general reluctance for the plant to put on new growth. When eelworm has been confirmed the best response on the part of the greenhouse owner is to burn the plant and the mix, and thoroughly to sterilize and clean around the area in which the plant was growing.

Cyclamen mite also attacks saintpaulias, is very difficult to detect and cannot be destroyed with available insecticides. Badly distorted leaves and flowers are an indication of their presence, and once this has been established it is advisable to burn all affected plants in order to prevent spread of this lethal pest. However, it must be added that in recent years in the commercial field this pest has not been so prevalent, and this usually implies that the situation is similar elsewhere.

Symphalids get the common name of springtails from the way in which they dance around on the soil of the pot when disturbed, and are usually in attendance when the growing mix is badly drained and, consequently, on the sour side. But they seem to do little harm and can be got rid of by watering BHC or malathion into the mix.

Sciarid fly is similar in that it exists in dank, badly ventilated greenhouse, but does little or no harm to plants. However, their presence does

Capsid bug damage to chrysanthemum

indicate that the gravel under the staging and on the staging should be raked over and the path washed down with a mild solution of disenfectant when the vents are likely to be open for several hours to get rid of the resultant smell. These flies are also more commonly referred to as fungus gnats and rise in clouds when one walks along the path of the greenhouse where the conditions are a little less than sweet. Diseases in the greenhouse are more often than not the result of indifferent culture, so you could say that the owner of the garden greenhouse is to some degree responsible for many of the problems that exist.

Overcrowding

From personal experience, one of the major difficulties in the small house is lack of space for all the many plants that are acquired at an almost alarming rate and, more so, the extreme reluctance on the part of the owner to have a spring clean and thin out the surplus. The result is that plants are packed in ever more tightly, with the inevitable stagnating conditions that exist around the pots as a result of little or no air being able to circulate. Such conditions become an ideal breeding ground for all manner of fungal problems that are very difficult to clear up while the indifferent cultural conditions exist. So the first exercise in fighting diseases in the greenhouse is to give plants room to breathe—this will reduce possibility of infection, and make any spraying programme more effective.

Botrytis is one of the fungus diseases that gets its first foothold in the greenhouse as a result of unhygienic conditions—botrytis will usually first attack rotting leaves and flowers around the plant before air-borne spores find their way onto living tissues. A wide range of plants are vulnerable to botrytis, and the congested leaf stalks of cyclamen plants present an ideal breeding ground. There are a number of preventative treatments, and Benomyl applied every seven days over three weeks is one of the best. Prevention is the best policy, however, and this will mean frequent inspection of your plants so that any dead or dying material can be completely removed—any tiny pieces of rotting stem or leaf that remain can prove fatal.

Mildew is a term used to describe a number of similar fungal diseases, and is seen as white powdery patches on the leaves of many ornamental and edible plants—again it is more prevalent where the greenhouse conditions tend to be dank

Scale insect damage on an aphelandra

and badly ventilated. There are many effective chemical treatments, but it is important to notice any attack early on, long before it has had a chance to become established. In fact it is wise to take the precaution of periodically dusting the greenhouse with a light treatment of one of the recommended deterrents. We hear of all sorts of treatments for the cure of plant problems, and not so long ago a dear old soul approached me at the end of a talk and said she cured mildew on her *Begonia rex* by dabbing the affected area with spittle. Not having tried it I cannot vouch for the remedy, and one could not imagine treating more than the odd plant in this odd and perhaps unhygienic way!

Root problems

Root diseases account for the failure of many more plants than you might imagine, and again the principal cause of the bother is cultural. This time it results from the mix in the pot becoming much too wet and remaining wet to the point whereby the roots in the pot begin to rot and die, with the result that the plant in time begins to wilt and possibly succumb. Clean sterilized growing mix that is well aerated and well drained is one of the best methods of preventing damage to the roots of greenhouse plants.

Another problem that may occur in respect of

roots is root knot eelworm which is seen as irregular swellings on the roots of the plant; plants can be treated by immersing their roots in boiling water, but it is really much more sensible to burn all badly affected plants and to isolate any that you are suspicious of. By isolating plants until a definite decision can be made there will be less likelihood of contaminating other clean plants.

Damping off of young seedlings can be a frustrating problem as they rot at soil level and keel over. Watering in Cheshunt Compound will help, but again the emphasis should be placed on cultural conditions that are warm, light and airy and careful watering that ensures that the growing medium is moist but not sodden.

Rust has already been mentioned as a comparatively modern scourge of chrysanthemums, in particular white rust which is causing so much concern among chrysanthemum growers and for which there is little protection at present. The dedicated chrysanthemum grower would be well advised to put his, or her plants into quarantine, as it is possible for anyone with infected plants to transmit the disease on their clothing. However proud you may be of your beautiful 'mums it could well be the best policy to leave the savouring of showing them off until they get to the show bench! (And you may wish to have yourself disinfected before returning from the show to your own plant collection.) Brown rust has been with us very much longer and is seen as raised brown spots on the leaves, and can be treated with thiram spray. All badly affected leaves should be destroyed at once.

Blossom end rot causes dark discolouration of tomato fruits, and is caused through erratic watering, in the same way as tomatoes will split when there are periods of drought between flooding with water. Discoloured fruit should be removed and disposed of.

There follows, in chart form, many of the problems that one is likely to encounter and recommended treatments, but it is again emphasized that the best policy is one of prevention. This means conditions that are as near right as possible for the particular plants being grown, clean and airy conditions, and watering and feeding that is done with care and not with abandon.

CROP, PLANT OR GREENHOUSE	DISORDERS	SYMPTOMS	PREVENTION AND CONTROL
General propagation, seed sowing, rooting cuttings, culture of young plants, bedding plants, etc.	Damping off; Pythium spp; Rhizocotonia spp., Phytophthora spp.	Base of seedlings and young plants turns light brown and stem constricts. Plant eventually collapses. Cuttings attacked in area of cut part or at compost level.	Cheshunt compound can be used before sowing and also for newly-germinated seedlings. Zineb or quintozene (PCNB) can also be used, as instructed on product, as can captan dust or spray
General propagation, seed sowing, rooting cuttings, culture of young plants, bedding plants, etc.	Grey mould	Attacks cuttings or young plants. Starts as light brown lesion, eventually becoming covered with grey dust-like spores	Again encouraged by high humidity. Especially troublesome in a greenhouse which is allowed to chill overnight. Use Thiram dust as directed on product, Captan or Tecnazene dust
Bulbs and corms; Carnations, chrysanthemums, cucumbers, pot plants, tomatoes, lettuce, peaches, nectarines, and crops in general	Aphids of various species. Small flies can be seen on leaves, usually in clusters	Attack leaves, feeding on plant sap, causing distortion and loss of vigour. Virus disease can also be transmitted by various species	Use insecticidal spray or atomizing fluid or smoke at first sign of attack, changing the nature of the chemical frequently, if possible, to avoid build up of resistance. Malathion, nicotine, derris gamma BHC, Dimethcate, Formothion, Menazon, are the main chemicals used. The last three are all systemics
Bulbs and corms; chrysanthemums, tomatoes, and several other crops	Caterpillars; Angle shade moth; Tomato moth	Caterpillars feeding on leaves and flowers, often at night	Gamma BHC smokes and sprays Cabaryil Fenitrothion and Trichlorphon sprays
Bulbs and corms; chrysanthemums	Stem eelworm (Ditylenchus dipsaci) attacks bulbs and other plants. Chrysanthemums attacked by specific eelworm (Apelenchoides ritzems-bosi)	Attack leaves and flowers causing distortion. In chrysanthemums brown blotches are formed on leaves, changing from yellow to bronze and purple	Destroy stock of bulbs and use only fresh soil in future. Chrysanthemums stools can be hot water treated—115°F for 5 minutes

CROP, PLANT OR GREENHOUSE	DISORDERS	SYMPTOMS	PREVENTION AND CONTROL
Narcissus (daffodils)	Narcissus flies	Eggs laid in or near bulbs in spring. Produce larvae which tunnel into bulbs, resulting in failure after planting	Bulb suppliers generally ensure that all bulbs are free from infestation by hot water treatment or chemical dipping
Narcissus (daffodils)	Leaf scorch (Stagonospora curtisii)	Leaf tip turns reddish brown, followed by death	Spray with Zineb at first sign of attack and repeat several times
Bulbs and corms; Carnations, chrysanthemums, cucumbers, pot plants generally, tomatoes inside shrubs	Thrips of various species, small brown or yellowish insects	Attack plants in various ways—sucking sap from leaves or flowers, causing acute distortion of growth. Silvery spots often show, especially on carnations. Breeding is more or less continuous	BHC smoke varied with Derris, Malathion and Nicotine, applied repeatedly until control is gained
Carnations, chrysanthemums, lettuce, tomatoes	Wireworms (small $\frac{1}{2}$–$\frac{3}{4}$in yellow-bodied insects)	Eggs laid in May/July. Larvae hatch in a few weeks and eat roots of plants. Persist for 4–5 years	Apply BHC (Gamma) as soil dust
Caranations, tomatoes	Fusarium wilt (Fusarium oxysporum and F. dianthi and other species)	Carnations and tomatoes are affected in warm areas. Plant wilt badly	Use clean stock and sterilized soil. Use Zineb when disease first appears
All crops	Grey mould (Bortrytis cinerea)	Attacks a wide range of plants, causing discoloration of leaves, followed by grey dust-like mould. Spreads extremely rapidly. Tomatoes badly attacked on stems, leaves or fruit. Ghost spot on fruit is caused by partial development of bortrytis. Lettuce can also be badly attacked	Keep atmosphere dry by skilful ventilation and application of heat. Avoid severe night temperature drops. Thiram dust or TCNB smoke should be used with care according to directions. Alternatively use Dicloran, Zineb or Benomyl (systemic)
Carnations	Carnation fly	Eggs laid on upper surface of leaves, resulting in larvae which moves into the stem	BHC smokes and sprays
Tulips	'Fire' (Botrytis tulipae)	Deformed shoots, followed by grey spots which eventually run together, resulting in reddish discoloration of leaves	Zineb, Thiram or Quintozene (PCNB) sprays or dust used at first sign of attack and persisted with
Many crops and plants	Earwigs	Bite holes in uowers and stems during night, causing acute distortion and malformation	Trap with inverted pots, and spray or dust with Gamma BHC
Many crops and plants	Red Spider Mite (Tetranychus urticae and T. cinnebarinus)	Nymphs and adults suck sap from leaves, causing yellowing and eventual destruction of leaves. Webs develop on underside of leaves, hindering control	Extremely persistent pests, over-wintering in cracks in greenhouse. A variety of materials should be used as smokes or sprays to avoid building up resistance. These include azo-benzene, derris, petroleum oil, Malathion and pormothion
Carnations, chrysanthemums, pot plants, shrubs	Powdery mildew (Oidium sp.)	Dirty white powder on leaves, stems and flowers	Dinocap spray or dust at first sign of attack
Carnations, chrysanthemums, and other plants	Rust (Uromyces dianthi)	Small blotches on leaves, later releasing reddish brown spores	Thiram, Zineb sprays or dusts, at first sign of disease. Overwinters in stools of chrysanthemums
Carnations	Stem rot (Fusarium culmorum) Verticillium wilt (Verticillium cinerescens)	Soil borne disease enters roots and spreads up plant, affecting moisture conducting tissue. Wilt follows, sometimes only on one side of plant on carnations	Adequate soil sterilization by heat or effective chemicals. Raising greenhouse temperature to 75°F for a week, combined with surface mulching, can offset trouble. Watering with Zineb is reasonably effective

CROP, PLANT OR GREENHOUSE	DISORDERS	SYMPTOMS	PREVENTION AND CONTROL
Tomatoes	Verticillium wilt (Verticillium alboatrum)		
Chrysanthemums	Gall midge (Diarthronomyia chrysanthemi)	Cone-shaped galls form on leaves and stems	Spray with gamma BHC at first sign of attack
Chrysanthemums, lettuce	Stool miner (Paila nigricornis)	Larvae feed on stem base and destroy cutting material	Spray with gamma BHC or Trichlophon spring and summer to destroy eggs.
Chrysanthemums, pot plants, tomatoes	Leaf miner (Phytomyza and Liriomyza solani)	Eggs laid on leaves produce larvae which tunnel into leaves	Gamma BHC aerosol, Gamma BHC smoke, when attack first noticed, or Trichlorphon spray
Chrysanthemums	Tarnished plant bug or capsid (Lygus rugulipennis)	Bugs suck sap, exuding toxin which twists and distorts. A wide range of plants are attacked out of doors	Malathion sprays, Gamma BHC smokes or sprays and Fenitrothion sprays
Chrysanthemums, cucumbers, melons, pot plants, tomatoes	White Fly (Trialeurodes vaporariorum)	Eggs laid on leaves, hatching into nymphs which suck sap and exude honeydew on which moulds develop. Growth is distorted. In pelargoniums leaf spot may be spread by this pest	A variety of sprays, dusts, aerosols, or smokes can be used, based on, Gamma BHC, Malathion, Pyrethrum or Derris. All must be used within 14 days and at short intervals to ensure control. Thorough cleaning or fumigating of greenhouse in winter when empty is essential
Chrysanthemums	Blotch or leaf spot (Spetoria chrysanthemella)	Grey or black blotches on leaves, often confused with eelworm	Spray with Zineb
Chrysanthemums	Petal damping, botrytis, grey mould	'Pin-pointing' of flower, followed by complete flower rot	Improve environment by application of heat, especially at night. TCNB smoke can be used at first sign of attack
Chrysanthemums	Petal blight (Itersonilia spp.)	Affects outside petals as water spots and spreads into flower centre	Zineb spray or dust before bud bursting
Chrysanthemums	Ray blight (Mycosphaerella ligulicola)	Mainly attacks inside when growing chrysanthemums on year round culture	Obtain clean stock. Spray with Zineb. Difficult to control once in existence
Cucumber	French fly (Tyrophagus sp.)	Introduced on straw (bales or loose). Mites feed on growing plant and leaves causing pale spots which later develop into holes. Usually disappear in high summer	Nicotine smokes or sprays
Cucumbers, melons, tomatoes	Leaf hoppers (Erythroneura pallidifrons)	Lively insects feeding on leaves cause distortion and restrict growth	Nicotine, malathion or Fenuitrothion at first sign of attack
Cucumber	Fungus gnats of various species	Develop initially on decaying fungi, FYM, or straw bales. Attack roots of plants causing wilting or death	Malathion watered into bed or use Gamma BHC drench
Cucumbers, melons and other soft plants	Springtails of various species	White six-legged soil pests feeding on soft stems, roots and root hairs in clusters. Some actively jump by means of tails	Gamma BHC drenches or dusts
Cucumbers, melons, lettuce, tomatoes and practically all other plants	Symphylid (Scutigerella immaculata)	Very active ¼in long insects feeding on roots, causing hard or deformed growth. They move down to lower depths of soil in winter or when soil is wet. Worst in highly organic soil	Thoroughly sterilize soil by heat or effective chemicals, Malathion drenches can be reasonably effective

CROP, PLANT OR GREENHOUSE	DISORDERS	SYMPTOMS	PREVENTION AND CONTROL
Cucumbers, tomatoes and other plants	Woodlice of various species	Attack plant roots or stems at soil level with drastic effects if in large numbers	Bait with cut turnips, Gamma BHC
Cucumbers	Black rot (Mycosphaerella citrullina)	Dieback of laterals at main stem. Identified by small black spots	Zineb spray, coupled with sterilization of boxes, etc. to avoid further spread of infection
Cucumbers	Gummosis (Cladosporium cucumerinum)	Silver spots on fruit which turn gummy, followed by velvety growth of green fungus	Zineb dust at first sign of attack
Cucumbers	Mildew (Erysiphe cichoracearum)	White felt over leaves	Dinocap spray or Beromyl systemic
Lettuce and other crops	Leatherjackets, various species	Tough leathery looking grubs, ½–1in long, feed on roots	Gamma BHC or Carbaryl dusts before planting. Can be very troublesome on new soils
Lettuce	Millipedes, various species	Many-legged 1in long creatures attacking roots and stems	Normally feed on organic matter. Adequate soil sterilization with Gamma BHC is most effective; or use Carbaryl dust
Lettuce, pot plants	Downy mildew (Bremia lactucae and other species)	Yellow areas on upper surface of leaves with grey fungus on correspondingly lower areas	Zineb dust at first sign of attack or Beromyl dust. Thiram system spray
Pot plants, peaches, nectarines, vines	Mealy bug (Pseudococcus spp.)	Little bugs covered with waxy secretion cluster on plants and cause distortion or loss of vigour, followed by leaf loss	Nicotine or malathion sprays and dusts. Methylated sprit applied directly to vine stems or peach branches is effective. Menazon system is also effective
Primulas, auriculas, lettuce	Root aphis (Pemphigus auriculae and other sp.)	Clusters of waxy-like insects present on the roots	Gamma BHC or nicotine drench
Vines, cyclamens and other plants	Vine weevil (Otiorrhynchus sulcatus)	Eggs laid in soil hatch in 2–3 weeks and white grubs feed on roots, causing wilting	Add Gamma BHC to compost if in doubt, or Gamma BHC drench at first sign of attack
Cyclamen	Root and corn rots (Cylindrocarpon radicola and Thielviopsis basicoli)	Soil borne disease which attacks and rots corms and roots of cyclamen	Use sterilized compost. Zineb drench is also effective
Tomatoes	Potato root eelworm (Heterodera rostochiensis)	Resting cysts start early in season releasing minute larvae which attack root systems, causing browning of lower leaves and wilting of plant. Their activities allow entry of root rots and other diseases	Very difficult to gain complete control in tomato borders. Alternative methods of cultivation allowing isolation from borders, using sterilized media, are advisable in bad cases. Dagomet granules give partial control
Tomatoes	Root-knot eelworm (Meloidogyne spp.)	Roots attacked, resulting in a deformed and galled appearance. Will rest in soil for 2 years in absence of host plants	Use metham/sodium sterilants. Failing this, adopt alternative cultural methods
Tomatoes	Buckeye rot	Soil borne spores splash on to fruit causing disfiguring dark brown rings	Take great care when watering, avoid splashing. Adequate ventilation will also help. Spray with Zineb at first sign of attack
Tomatoes	Didymella stem rot (Didymella lycopersici)	Attacks plants at soil level, causing brown-grey sunken lesions which extend up the stem, eventually girdling it, killing plants. Shiny spores may be seen on detailed examination with a lens	Sterilize house thoroughly in winter and get rid of infected haulms well away from greenhouse. Paint bottom of stem with dithane at first sign of attack, and sterilize soil thoroughly by heat

CROP, PLANT OR GREENHOUSE	DISORDERS	SYMPTOMS	PREVENTION AND CONTROL
Tomatoes	Leaf mould (Cladosporium fulvum)	Starts as yellow spots on upper surface, with corresponding grey-brown mould patches on lower surfaces. Appearance of disease coincides with periods of still muggy weather, when humidity is high. Once established it can spread rapidly and affect flowers as well as leaves. Has an overall yield-reducing effect	Certain districts are notorious for this disease, especially those where humidity is high. It is always advisable to grow resistant varieties in bad areas. When non-resistant varieties are grown, spray with copper, zineb in season. TCNB smokes can also be used. Good ventilation night and day, coupled with adequate air movement by means of fans or use of heaters, will do much to offset the trouble
Tomatoes	Potato blight (Phytophthora infestans)	More common in the south where tomatoes are grown out of doors. Brown sunken areas appear on fruit	The same control measures as described for leaf mould should be practised
Tomatoes	Root and foot rot (Phytophthora spp.; Pythium spp., Rhizoctonia solani)	Fungi enter through roots or base of stem, especially when plants are subjected to growing checks or soils are unusually wet or previously badly contaminated	Soil sterilization for the future is essential. Zineb can be used at 3–4 week intervals. Avoid checks to growth (especially planting in cold soil)
Tomatoes	Sclerotinia disease (Sclerotinia sclerotiorum)	Only base of stems attacked. A white mould develops, followed by black resting bodies. Plants wilt and die	Special attention should be paid to sterilization for the future
PHYSIOLOGICAL DISORDERS			
TOMATOES	Blossom end rot	End of fruit develops a black zone	This is caused by inadequate or irregular watering or too high a salt content
	Cracking or splitting of fruit	Where fruit cracks or splits	Due to widely varying environmental conditions and may largely be influenced by type of weather
	Dry set and blossom drop	Where flowers fall off or fruit fails to set	Due again to irregular growing conditions, especially temperatures below 65°F and above 80°F, also perhaps to virus infection
	Blotchy ripening	Irregular ripening of fruit	Caused by day temperatures being too high and by irregular feeding. Go onto regular liquid feeds and keep potash level high
POT PLANTS	Over-watering	Yellowing and wilting of lower leaves	Always ensure that plants are not over-watered by constant supervision. Sometimes low night temperature has the same effect
MANY PLANTS	Over-feeding	Scorched appearance of foliage and leaf tips	Apply less feeding or in more diluated form
	Gross lanky length	Lack of light	Make sure that plants obtain maximum light, especially in winter, bearing in mind their likes and dislikes in this direction

Appendix

Brand names of chemicals	Chemical Ingredient	Manufactuerer
Abol Derris Dust	Derris	ICI
Abol X Greenfly Killer	Menazon	ICI
Ant Destroyer	Gamma BHC	Boots
Ant Doom	Derris	UGS
Anti-Ant Powder	Pyrethrum	Pan Britannica Industries
Ant Killer	Gamma BHC	Doff
Ant Killer Liquid	Chlordane	Murphy
Ant Killer Powder	Chlordane	Murphy
Ant Powder	Pyrethrum	Corry
Bioresmethrin	Bioresmethrin	Kyldane
Bio Sprayday	Resmethrin, pyrethrum	Pan Britannica Industries
Bromophos	Bromophos	Pan Britannica Industries
Combat Garden Insecticide	Dimethoate, gamma BHC, malathion	Fisons
Combat Slug Pellets	Metaldehyde	Fisons
Combat Soil Insecticide	Diazinon	Fisons
Combat Whitefly Insecticide	Bioresmethrin	Fisons
Combined Pest and Disease Dust	Derris, malathion, sulphur, zineb	Murphy
Combined Seed Dressing	Captan, gamma BHC	Murphy
Compound Quassia Extract	Quassia	Bentley
Crop Saver	Malathion, trichlorphon	Pan Britannica Industries
Derris Dust	Derris	Boots Corry Doff Murphy UGS
Derris Insecticide	Derris	Bentley
Dipterex	Trichlorphon	May & Baker
Draza Slug Pellets	Methiocarb	May & Baker
Fentro	Fenitrothion	Murphy
Gamma BHC Cone	Gamma BHC	Fumite
Gamma BHC Dust	Gamma BHC	Murphy
Garden Insecticide	Diazinon	Ciba-Geigy
Garden Insect Killer	Gamma BHC, pyrethrum, piperonyl butoxide	Boots
Garden Insect Killer	Pyrethrum	Py Spray Company
Garden Insect Powder	Carbaryl	Boots
Greenfly Killer	Malathion	Boots
Greenhouse Aerosol	Malathion	Murphy

Brand names of chemicals	Chemical Ingredient	Manufacturer
Hexyl Plus	Gamma BHC, Derris, Thiram	Pan Britannica Industries
House Plant Pest Killer	Pyrethrum	Synchemicals
Jeyes Fluid		Jeyes
Kerispray House Plant Insect Killer	Pyrethrum, pirimiphos methyl	ICI
Kilsect	Trichlorphon	Pan Britannica Industries
Leaf Miner Insecticide	Nicotine	Bentley
Lindex Garden Spray	Gamma BHC	Pan Britannica Industries
Lindonc	Gamma BHC	Fumite
Lindone	Gamma BHC	Kyldane
Liquid Derris	Derris	Murphy Pan Britannica Industries
Liquid Malathion	Malathion	Murphy
Malathion Dust	Malathion	Murphy
Mealy Bug Destroyer	Pyrethrum, methylated spirits	Corry
Mortegg	Tar Oil	Murphy
Murfume BHC Smoke	Gamma BHC	Murphy
Murfume Lindone Smoke Pellets	Gamma BHC	Murphy
Naled	Naled	Kyldane
New Garden Insecticide	Pyrethrum, Gamma BHC	Carters
Nicotine	Nicotine	Kyldane
Nicotine Fibre	Nicotine	Bentley
Nicotine Insecticide	Nicotine	Bentley
Nippon	Chlordane, pyrethrum	Synchemicals
Nippon Ant Destroyer	Borax	Synchemicals
Nippon Ant Powder	Chlordane	Synchemicals
Orchid Insecticide	Nicotine	Bentley
Ovamort Special	DNOC, petroleum oil	Murphy
Panant	Disodium tetraborate	Pan Britannica Industries
Plant Pest Killer	Pyrethrum	Synchemicals
Premier Plant Spray	Methylated Spirit	Bentley
Pydercite	Pyrethrum	Bentley
Pyrethrum Powder	Pyrethrum	Corry
Quassia Extract	Quassia	Corry
Racumin	Coumatetralyl	Pan Britannica Industries
Rapid Greenfly Killer	Pirimicarb	ICI
Root Guard	Diazinon	Ciba-Geigy
Sevin Dust	Carbaryl	Murphy
Slug Death	Metaldehyde	Corry
Slug Destroyer	Metaldehyde	Bentley
Slug Destroyer	Metaldehyde	Boots
Slug Guard	Methiocarb	Pan Britannica Industries
Slugit Pellets	Metaldehyde	Murphy
Slug Killer Pellets	Metaldehyde	Carters
Slug Mini-pellets	Metaldehyde	Pan Britannica Industries
Sluoids	Metaldehyde	Doff
Soil Pest Killer	Chlorophyriphos	Murphy
Soluble Paraffin Oil	Paraffin Oil	Bentley
Spidacide	Fusil Oil	Bentley
Sybol 2	Pyrethrum	ICI
Systemic Greenfly Gun	Oxydemeon methyl	May & Baker
Systemic Insecticide	Dimethoate	Murphy
Tecnalin	Gamma BHC, tecnazene	Fumite
Tip-Top Slug Pellets	Metaldehyde	Doff
Tugon Ant Killer	Trichlorphon	May & Baker
Warfarin	Warfarin	Murphy
Wasp Destroyer	Gamma BHC	Corry
Wasp Destroyer	Carbaryl	Murphy
XL All Insecticide	Nicotine	Synchemicals

ALUMINIUM FRAMES

Alitex Ltd
Station Road, Alton, Hants
Alton Glasshouses Ltd
PO Box 3, Bewdley, Worcs
Aluminium Greenhouses Ltd
Aluminium House, 68/72 Wednesfield Road, Little London, Willenhall, Staffs
Aluz Aluminium Greenhouses,
Market Square, Bampton, Oxon
Baco Leisure Products Ltd
Glebe Road, Huntingdon, Cambridge
Banbury Buildings Ltd
PO Box 11, Banbury, Oxon
Cambridge Glasshouse Co Ltd
Barton Road, Comberton, Cambridge
Cases Greenhouses Ltd
Forest Road, Taffs Well, Cardiff
Clearspan Ltd
Wellington Road, Greenfield, Oldham, Lancs
Compton Buildings
Station Works, Fenny Compton, Leamington Spa, Warks
Cramphorn Ltd
Cuton Mill, Chelmsford, Essex
Crittal Warmlife Ltd
Crittal Road, Witham, Essex
Edenlite Ltd
Hawksworth, Swindon, Wilts
Europa Manor Engineers Ltd
Oxford Road, Brackley, Northants
Florada Ltd
2 Church Street, Fen Ditton, Cambridge
Garden Craft Ltd
Sutton-on-Trent, Newark, Notts
Gardener Buildings Ltd
Plough Farm, Forton Road, Newport, Salop
Guildhall Garden Products Ltd
Guild House, Hearsall Lane, Earlsdon, Coventry
Guernsey Glasshouses Ltd
Braye Road Industrial Estate, Vale, Guernsey
Halls Homes & Gardens Ltd
Church Road, Paddock Wood, Kent
Harry Hebdith Ltd
Martock, Somerset
Humex Ltd
High Road, Weybridge, Surrey
Kenkast Ltd
Chaddock Lane, Astley, Manchester
Kingston Developments Ltd
PO Box 90, Kingston-upon-Hull, Yorks
Marley Greenhouses Ltd
Chantry Lane, Storrington, Sussex
Edward Owen Engineering Ltd
Newman Lane, Alton, Hants
Paradise Ltd
15 Stratton Heights, Cirencester, Glos
Pratten Greenhouses
Midsomer Norton, Bath
Qualcast Ltd
Coleridge Street, Sunnyhill, Derby
Robinsons of Winchester Ltd
Robinson House, Winchester
Royal Greenhouses
PO Box 3, Bewdley, Worcs
Simplex Ltd
Sawston, Cambridge
Springvale Garden Greenhouses
Neville House, Waterloo Street, Birmingham
Sun Aluminium Greenhouses
Reliance Works, Navigation Road, Chelmsford, Essex
Tropical Greenhouses
Unit 4, Junction 34, Greabrough Road, Tinsley, Sheffield

WOODEN FRAMES

Alton Glasshouses Ltd
PO Box 3, Bewdley, Worcs
Banbury Buildings Ltd
PO Box 11, Banbury, Oxon
Barratts Buildings Ltd
Longdowns, Nr Penrhyn, Cornwall
Cookson Portable Buildings
298 Alcester Road, Moseley, Birmingham
Cotswold Buildings
Cotswold Works, Standlake, Nr Witney, Oxon
Davies & Clifford Ltd
Star Road, Hillingdon Heath, Middlesex
William Gregory & Son Ltd
Joinery Works, The Cliff, Tansley, Matlock, Derby
Halls Homes & Gardens Ltd
Church Road, Paddock Wood, Kent
Harry Hebdith Ltd
Martock, Somerset
Janes & Green Ltd
Guildford Road, St Albans, Herts
Kenkast Ltd
Chaddock Lane, Astley, Manchester
L. F. Knight Ltd
Reigate Heath, Reigate, Surrey
Lewes Road Sawmills Ltd
Glencoe, Scaynes Hill, Sussex
Page Sectional Buildings Ltd
Coral Street, Saltburn by Sea, Cleveland
Pratten Greenhouses
Midsomer Norton, Bath
Rayners Buildings Ltd
Llanaway Works, Guildford Road, Godalming, Surrey
Regal Portable Buildings Ltd
Langley Mill, Nottingham
Royal Greenhouses
PO Box 3, Bewdley, Worcs
Silver Mist Ltd
Reliant Works, Brockham, Betchworth, Surrey
G. F. Strawson Ltd
St Andrews Works, Charlesfield Road, Horley, Surrey
C. A. Sydenham-Hannaford Ltd
Hamworth Junction, Poole, Dorset
E. C. Walton & Co Ltd
Sutton on Trent, Newark, Lincs
C. H. Whitehouse Ltd
Buckhurst Works, Frant, Sussex

PLASTIC, POLYTHENE, ETC

Agriframes Ltd
Charlswood Road, East Grinstead, Sussex
Bluehart Ltd
139a High Street, Wootton Basset, Wilts
Clovis Lande Associates Ltd
Gaza Trading Estate, Weald, Hildenborough, Kent
Flexipane Ltd
Priory Works, Newton Street, Newton St Faith, Norwich, Norfolk
Garden Relax Ltd
113 Wennington Road, Rainham, Essex
Growth Cell Products Ltd
11 Monmouth View, Llanbradach, Glamorgan
Jaybeam Ltd
Moulton Park Industrial Estate, Northampton
Joseph Paxton Ltd
36 Tooley Street, London E1
Refal Portable Buildings Ltd
Langley Mill, Nottingham
F. J. Saunders & Co Ltd
Lime Kiln Lane, Thetford, Norfolk
Simplex Ltd
Sawston, Cambridge
Transatlantic Plastics Ltd
Garden Estate, Ventnor, Isle of Wight

METRIC AND OTHER CONVERSION FACTORS

DEFINITION	TO CONVERT	INTO	MULTIPLY BY
Temperature rise	deg F	deg C	0.55
and fall	deg C	deg F	1.8
Length	in	mm	25.4
	mm	in	0.0394
	ft	metres (m)	0.3048
	m	ft	3.2808
Area	ft^2	m^2	0.0929
	m^2	ft^2	10.7639
Volume	ft^3	m^3	0.0283
	m^3	ft^3	35.3148
Mass	lb	kg	0.4536
	kg	lb	2.2046

BUILDING HEAT LOSS DATA

THERMAL TRANSMITTANCE:

U-value		
Btu/ft^2 deg F	W/m^2 deg C	5.678
W/m^2 deg C	Btu/ft^2 deg F	0.176

Useful data:

20 fluid ounces = 1 pint = 0.56 l
1 gallon of water weighs 10lb/4.5kg
1 litre of water weighs 2.216/.9kg
Cubic capacity is calculated by multiplying length × breadth × average height

TEMPERATURE CONVERSION TABLE

°F	°C	°F	°C	°F	°C
86	30.0	60	15.6	34	1.1
85	29.4	59	15.0	33	0.6
84	28.9	58	14.4	32	0.0
83	28.3	57	13.9	31	− 0.6
82	27.8	56	13.3	30	− 1.1
81	27.2	55	12.8	29	− 1.7
80	26.7	54	12.2	28	− 2.2
79	26.1	53	11.7	27	− 2.8
78	25.6	52	11.1	26	− 3.3
77	25.0	51	10.6	25	− 3.9
76	24.4	50	10.0	24	− 4.4
75	23.9	49	9.4	23	− 5.0
74	23.3	48	8.9	22	− 5.6
73	22.8	47	8.3	21	− 6.1
72	22.2	46	7.8	20	− 6.7
71	21.7	45	7.2	19	− 7.2
70	21.1	44	6.7	18	− 7.8
69	20.6	43	6.1	17	− 8.3
68	20.0	42	5.6	16	− 8.9
67	19.4	41	5.0	15	− 9.4
66	18.9	40	4.4	14	−10.0
65	18.3	39	3.9	13	−10.6
64	17.8	38	3.3	12	−11.1
63	17.2	37	2.8	11	−11.7
62	16.7	36	2.2	10	−12.2
61	16.1	35	1.7		

Formulae for conversion: Celsius to Fahrenheit = (°C × 1.8) + 32
Fahrenheit to Celsius = (°F − 32) × .55

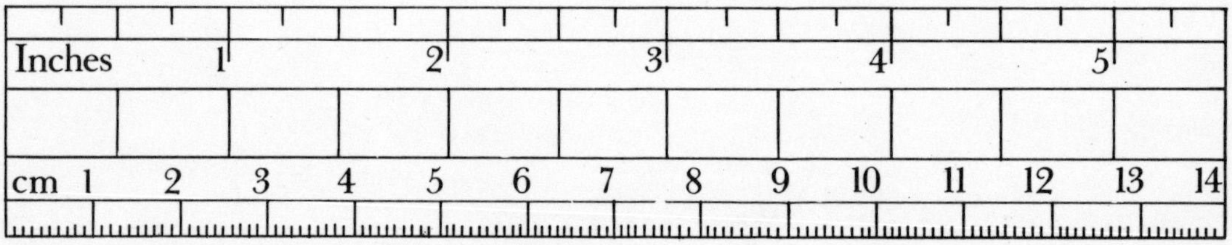

Index